YOU'RE NOT

BEHIND

DISCOVERING PURPOSE IN

THE DELAY

YOU'RE NOT

BEHIND

DISCOVERING PURPOSE IN

THE DELAY

David D. Roberson

Maximized Productions, LLC. – UPH Publishing Div.

You're Not Behind copyright © 2019 by David D. Roberson

Published by Maximized Productions, LLC. UPH Publishing Div..

6715 Suitland Rd. – Morningside, MD 20746

www.maximizedproductions.com

701-484-3303

All rights reserved. No part of this publication may be reproduced, stored in a retrieval system, or transmitted in any form by any mean, electronic mechanical, photocopy, recording, or otherwise, without the prior permission of the publisher, except as provided for by USA copyright law.

ISBN: 978-1-7327503-6-4

Please direct your inquiries to the address above or visit:

www.maximizedproductions.com or

www.ddrministries.org

Cover Design by Daniel Newman of SaltedRootsStudio.com

Photo by John "Jai" Chatmon of 1001Words

www.500px.com/jchatmonii

First printing 2019 Printed in the USA

REVIEW

One of the greatest opportunities that has been presented to me is the privilege and honor to share with every person that reads this book, the Spiritual aptitude, unity of mind and, spirit of the Author.

What Pastor David has revealed is the reality of a maturing and committed relationship with He who knows us best. These collective writings will absolutely challenge the reader to evaluate the Truth about themselves. What captivates my heart is the "simplicity " and honesty revealed in the personal testimony of his journey.

If you do not know or never thought about your "purpose of life," then this book is a must-read. It is all-inclusive.

Only by the guidance and Anointing of the Holy Spirit could this book be written. It is beyond natural abilities. I feel that it is the Voice of God speaking through a surrendered servant whose heart has been tenderized by life's experiences.

My heart is lifted, and my soul delights in this body of work because the Author is my one and only Son, whom I love dearly. Thank you,
Pastor David Deon Roberson.

Pastor TJ Roberson, St. Paul Missionary Baptist Church

INTRODUCTION

One morning after dropping my daughters off at school, I began talking to God about my future. I wanted to know, "What next?" I wanted to know if I would ever be financially secure. I even asked God if I was doing what He wanted me to do. As I continued talking to Him, I begin to list all of the things I'd like to do but can't due to my responsibilities as a Pastor. I reminded Him of the sacrifices I'd made to walk and live in obedience to the call on my life.

As I continued speaking, 1st Corinthians 2:9 begin speaking in my spirit: But as it is written, "Eye hath not seen, nor ear heard, neither have entered into the heart of man, the things which God hath prepared for them that love him." I know I love God. I know God loves me. Instantly my level of expectation from God increased. I ask, God? What am I not doing? His response gave birth to the book you now hold that I pray will change your life. He said unto me:

"You're a writer. You think songs. I've prepared books, operating procedures, plans, scripts, messages, and songs. You've loved a portion of who you are because that portion is easier and seems more profitable. You've not yet tapped into everything I've placed in you."

I asked God, "Lord, if it's your will and my purpose to write more books than I already have, I need you to give me patience. I need you to open my mind. I need you to really touch my heart because this isn't something I've ever dreamt of." That same day, I sat and wrote the first four chapters of this book.

At the age of 46, having started life over at the age of 40 I too wrestled, and occasionally still wrestle with the thought of not being where I should be in life. However, God reminds me daily that every day has purpose, and I'm right where I should be in order to fulfill my destiny through Him.

You're not behind. Today is a good day to discover your purpose. Embrace today, and you'll realize that even your past steps were ordered by God. There is truly purpose behind every delay.

David D. Roberson

FOREWORD

Psalms 37:23 declares that the steps of a good man are ordered by the Lord and he delights in his way! This is a very amazing and important scripture to comprehend. Because it declares that the steps to the path of your life have already been determined. Which means that success in life is simply placing your feet in the footprints that God has already established for you.

In his book "You're Not Behind," Pastor David Roberson gives us clear understanding of not only how to discover your PURPOSE, but also how to skillfully and strategically walk out your PATH to it.

This book is the answer to the question that lies deep within the subconscious of every human born. Why am I here? Until this question is answered, the TRUE life that God has destined for you will never be realized. Because after all, if you don't know what you are BORN for, you will never truly know what to LIVE for.

Isaac Pitre
Christ Nations Church

TABLE OF CONTENTS

"WHAT IS PURPOSE?" 16
THE SUPPORT SYSTEM 22
I DID IT ON PURPOSE 29
MY WILL, I WILL. HIS WILL, HE WILL. 40
BECAUSE 48
YOU'RE NOT BEHIND 58
RELAY (PASS THE BATON) 69
UNINVITED 77
ANOINTED FOR THIS 86
TRANSITIONAL PHASE 97
UGLY PHASE 104
SUBMISSION 113
GOD'S NOT ANSWERING ME 118
YES? 125
PURPOSD CONEALED (STOP LEANING) 130
PURPOSE REVEALED 141

CHAPTER ONE

"WHAT IS PURPOSE?"

Ever said to yourself, "Is that it? There has to be more." At some point in your life, you began to wonder if you've been tricked or lied to about what life has to offer. I mean, you've done everything you thought you were supposed to do in order to set yourself up for a great future. You finished high school, graduated from college, took up a trade, landed a great paying job, got married, had children, and suddenly you felt like something was missing. You felt unfulfilled. You felt as though you took a wrong turn somewhere. People on the outside looking in would trade anything to walk in your shoes. However, what they fail to realize is that you feel as though you followed a script that was written out for you with you having very little input about how you wanted to develop the character that you would daily have to live out. You ask yourself, am I truly living out my purpose? Why do I feel empty?

There are times in life when we began to slow down and take inventory of where we are and what we've accomplished.

Often times we seek fulfillment in people, places, or things. People like spouses, children, or friends. Places like exotic vacations. Things like jobs, money, or material gain. Granted, these are really beautiful things to have, but many have discovered not even beautiful things can fill a void that is created by purpose.

The why of my existence is a question that drives many to begin the search for their true identity. Who am I? What am I here for? Or as the infamous King David would say in Psalm 8:3-4 (NIV),

When I consider your heavens, the work of your fingers, the moon and the stars, which you have set in place, WHAT IS MANKIND that you are mindful of them, human beings that you care for them?

What was God really saying when He spoke to Jeremiah, "Before I formed thee in the womb I knew you, before you were born I set you apart; I appointed you as a prophet to the

nations." (Jeremiah 1:5 NIV). He was saying before I formed you, I gave you purpose. I created you with an agenda. I created you to make a difference. I created you to make an impact. Before you were formed, a place in life has already been established and reserved for you. You do have a reason for being here. You are not a mistake. Regardless of how you arrived here, you arrived with a purpose already in you prior to your conception. You were formed around your purpose.

For some, the circumstances you were born in seemed to have put you behind because you've had to overcome obstacles that have slowed your pace or caused you to venture off in life. For most of us, some of the decisions we've made have led us down a road that seemed to have done more damage than good. Even after all of the rejection, misunderstandings, bad decisions, and insecurities, there's still something on the inside saying, "There's more to it than this." The question is, what are you going to do about the void?

What is purpose? The dictionary describes purpose as something set up as an object or end to be attained: Intention, Resolution, Determination. Or a subject under discussion or an action in course of execution. With all of that being understood, what is purpose? If it's ok, I'd like to pull from my own personal dictionary:

Purpose, is the reason why something or someone exists. The word reason in the Greek language is logos. Logos means "word" or "plan." When God spoke to Jeremiah (Jeremiah 29:11) He (God) said, "For I know the PLANS (REASON, PURPOSE) I have for you declares the Lord, "plans to prosper you and not harm you, PLANS (REASON, PURPOSE) to give you hope and a future. Remember Jeremiah 1:5 stated, "Before I formed you in the womb, I knew you, before you were born I set you apart; I appointed you as a prophet to the nations. Just for clarity, He's speaking directly to Jeremiah in regard to Jeremiah's calling. However, the same principle applies to us today. God is saying to us, "David (say your own name), Before I formed you in the womb, I was intimate with you. I knew you. I knew you before your parents knew each other. I already planned and purposed your life. PLANS (REASON, PURPOSE) to prosper you and give you hope and a future. I appointed you as a son, brother, husband, father, a singer, pastor, manager, chef, songwriter, author, counselor, preacher, teacher, speaker to the nations, faith walker, hand laying healer, death bed speaking, demon casting son of the Most High God. Now, if you included your name and everything you are or have become over the course of your life, you'll begin to see your purpose form right before your eyes.

There's absolutely nothing easy about trying to discover your purpose or your why. Discover simply means to look for and uncover (at least that's how I interpret it). What does that mean? It means it was already there. Many times, we grow discouraged or impatient with ourselves when seeking out our purpose because it causes us to dig. It causes us to admit that we may have been wrong and misled. I'm not here to lie to you and tell you that you will discover your purpose by the time you're finish reading this book. What I am here to tell you is how I began to discover mine. I am here to tell you that it's going to take some work, perseverance, and a commitment. It's your life, and you were created with a plan already written just for you. Why not take the time and discover what God already knows about you?

Power Points of Purpose:

CHAPTER TWO

THE SUPPORT SYSTEM

As consumers, we want the best out of every product we purchase. Some products have more value than others. It's no coincidence that products with the most value are often the most fragile. In most cases, at the time of purchase, an extended warranty is offered at an additional cost. Once the product is in our possession, there's a limited warranty that will cover certain things for a certain amount of time. Purchasing the extended warranty will increase the protective coverage. You receive more grace in the event something happens. Having the warranty doesn't give us the right to mistreat the product. In fact, if the product malfunctions and the warranty must be used, the manufacturer will examine the product to determine if the product has been abused. The word abuse was created by compounding two different words, abnormal and use. Should the manufacturer see where abuse or abnormal use has occurred, unless specified, the warranty will be voided. The manufacturer may deny the claims if it's determined that the product has been intentionally abused or used improperly. If the product has malfunctioned due to user error in the attempt to use correctly or even if the product has glitches that weren't identified prior to being sold, the maker will then apply the warranty. Do you see where we're headed? No God does not view us as products. We are His children and we have been designed with His DNA. We have been equipped by the best. But for sake of understanding, let's continue with this analogy.

God knew that prior to us being born into this world that we would be tampered with. We would, in some cases, be molded by the hands of other human beings who were molded themselves. He knew that we would experience times that would cause us to hate our very existence. He knew we would make mistakes that would lead us down a path of desolation. So, prior to our formation in the womb, He already had a PLAN (Reason, Purpose) for us. Because of what we've had to experience to get to this point, He, Jesus Christ Himself, purchased us with His precious blood and applied an extended warranty called Grace and Mercy to our lives.

We, or maybe it's just me and other people like me, attempt to put things together based on what we see. We want the quick fix. We lack the patience and at times the humility to put things together the way it was designed. We get in a hurry and make decisions in an effort to compete with or to impress others. Why?

In my home, my wife is Mrs. Fix it. She is the first to grab the Allen wrenches and socket sets. And there is absolutely no shame in my game. Recently we purchased a new home. With a new home comes new furniture. We purchased a new 55-inch OLED crystal clear screen TV. Prior to connecting the television, we needed a television stand that would be able to support the width and the weight of it. After walking the aisle at the store and looking at several different stands, I settled on one that would fit our color scheme. It also looked simple enough to put together in a few minutes. The cable man has already wired the house. The internet is up and running. I'm ready to plug in and get lost in the millions of colors the television had to offer. So, on the dolly, it goes. From the looks of it, there were only five to eight major steps. Of course, a few screws, washers, and knobs but that's a no brainer right. Once we got home and began to remove the pieces from the box, there were at least ten other parts that I couldn't see by looking at the picture on the outside of the box. There were four times as many screws and washers than I expected. We had to examine the screws to make sure we had the right sized Allen wrenches and screwdrivers to complete the job. Anyone that knows me knows that this is where I checked out. My wife is extremely detailed oriented and patient when it comes to these things. She removed all of the material from the box.

She separated all of the screws, she separated the washers, she separated the knobs, she separated the back panel from the front panel, she separated the doors, she separated the shelves, she separated the top cover from the base, you get the picture. Then she counted each piece to confirm what was written in the instructions. After confirming she had all of the parts, she then put the receipt in a place where she could find it in the event we needed to return the stand to the store. I was now assigned to make room in the living room for her to work. She and my daughter sat on the floor in what looked like a mess to me and read the instructions line by line and assembled the stand in the fashion that the maker intended.

In the past, I've put things together and had a hand full of screws left and swore that the manufacturer must've given us some extras. My wife would pleasantly ask, did you read the instructions? I'd pridefully say, "Nope!" I didn't realize is that being in a hurry to use a product will cause us to rush the process of putting it together. In Philippians 4:6, Paul said, "Do not be anxious about anything, but in every situation, by prayer and petition, with thanksgiving, present your request to God. What's the rush? Trying to put life together based on what others make it look like can cause you to misplace or leave out some key parts that may look small, but they keep things together.

Back to the TV stand, I didn't have a problem with my wife and my daughter taking half the day to put it together. I didn't have a problem making room for where it was going to go. I didn't have a problem doing other things around the house in order to stay out of the way. I realized the stand was the foundation needed in order to hold the new 55-inch super-thin OLED Television that was purchased (extended warranty added). The stand took more time to assemble but yet cost a fraction of what the tv cost. The stands monetary value is far less than the TV that it will securely support. But, the purpose of the stand is priceless. Had they put the stand together simply by looking at the picture, how reliable would the stand have been? It's possible the stand wouldn't be able to support the weight that we were planning to place on it had it not be securely and rightly put together (2 Timothy 2:15).

We are only as strong as our foundation. When our foundation is secure, God is able to unfold His PLAN (REASON, PURPOSE) in our lives. It's a fact that many of us have used a chair as a ladder because we didn't have a ladder readily available. What if while using the chair as a ladder, it folded? It was designed to be sat in, not stood on.

That is considered abnormal use, or abuse. Paul said in 1 Corinthians 10:23:

All things are legitimate permissible – and we are free to do anything we please, but not all things are helpful (expedient, profitable, and wholesome). All things are legitimate, but not all things are constructive to character and edifying to spiritual life.

I can do what I want, but not everything is beneficial to me. Not everything is beneficial to my purpose. I can take short cuts, but what am I leaving out that may be necessary to hold the weight of His PLAN (REASON, PURPOSE) for my life. The warranty is necessary but don't void it by taking short cuts.

Power Points of Purpose:

CHAPTER THREE

I DID IT ON PURPOSE

For many years of my life I believed that my purpose was solely wrapped in my talent. I thought because I grew up in a musical family, I was truly destined to grace many stages singing songs that I had written. I went from singing with the family group growing up to organizing and singing with a couple of R&B groups throughout my college and young adult years. I was so dedicated to making this my pathway to fame and fortune that I walked away from my college education and moved to Detroit on a promise that would never come to fruition. Because what I was doing felt right, I never once bothered to ask God if this was the plan He had for my life. I thought because I could sing, write, and perform, this must be the plan for my life. I'm going to be famous. I'm going to be rich. This is what I was created to do, so I thought. Before I go too far into this chapter, let me make it clear that I have no regrets of the road I took to get me back to this point. I learned a lot and had some pretty good times.

Over a 10-year period of my life, I committed to music. Not only did I leave college in Fall of 1996, I left my children there as well. I wanted so bad to be successful in music to where my priorities were music, music, music, self, music, family. I was raised listening to all of the stories of the sacrifices it took to be successful. I believed that one day, if I hit it big, I would be able to bring my children with me and take care of them the way I wanted to. I was so driven by the fuel of success to where I didn't realize that I was taking the road to destruction and possible eternal separation from my God and my family. I completely stopped going to church. I quit reading the bible. Growing up I was in church 5 to 7 times per week for what seemed like hours. In my mind I was finally free to be me, and no one was going to stop me in the pursuit of my dreams.

  I, like many people today, believed that my purpose was in my occupation. What's remarkable is nowadays I see more doctors, lawyers, and corporate executives walking away from years on the job because they found their true purpose in life. Can you imagine working for years in a field, making millions, and yet still feeling unfulfilled? I thought if I worked hard enough in my craft, I would eventually make it. The funny thing about that is, it's true! If you work hard at anything, eventually you will be successful at it. I hear you saying,

"What's wrong with that?" Absolutely nothing if you've operated in the principle of Proverbs 16:3 NIV

"Commit to the Lord whatever you do, and He will establish your path."

Let's think about something. God is the giver of the talent, right? God also allows us to choose how we use what He has given us, right? However, if you want the best out of what you've been given, wouldn't it be wise to commit to the one who gave it to you? Everything God gives us, has a purpose (PLAN, REASON) assigned to it. Sounds like the chair and ladder analogy from the previous chapter. Just because you can, doesn't always mean that you should.

As I continue pursuing my dreams of being a national recording artist, I realized that most of the people I drew closer to always had somewhere to be on Sundays, Church. So eventually I'd end up at someone's service on Sunday in Pontiac, Michigan just to hang out after service with friends.

One Sunday after a really spirit-filled service, I got back to our townhome and went to my room. I couldn't shake what I felt. It felt good. It felt home. It felt like something I'd been missing. Even though I grew up in church, this was something different. What I felt created an appetite. Over time I found myself growing distant from the guys I'd sang with for years. I became rude. I was irritable. I didn't want to be around anyone. No, I wasn't depressed. I even lost my desire to be around music. I was beginning to think that maybe this was a sign for me to begin another career, or try another direction. However, deep down I knew I was being separated.

Have you ever stuck with something because you'd invested a lifetime in to it, but your heart wasn't there? That's where I was. I was emotionally withdrawn from the very thing I sacrificed my family and my college education for. I shut down. Often my friends would reach out attempting to get me to open up, but they were unsuccessful. I knew I was going through something, but I just couldn't put what I was dealing with into words. So instead of trying to talk, I'd lash out and isolated myself from everyone. The only time I would find peace of mind was when I went to church.

One Wednesday night, I recall driving and screaming to the top of my lungs, "WHAT'S GOING ON WITH ME!" I was driving through a snowstorm. A song by Rev. Clay Evans came on the radio "I've Got A Testimony." I cried and sang that song to the top of lungs in my truck. Why? From my viewpoint, I'm a mess. What testimony do I have? I realize now that my spirit was rejoicing for what was getting ready to take place in the years to come. I couldn't understand why this song was so powerful considering I wasn't living the best life of a Christian. Nevertheless, I kept crying and singing.

I make known the end from the beginning, from ancient times, what is still to come. I say, "My purpose will stand, and I will do all that I please."

Before God starts, He's already finished. Isaiah 46:10 says:

It's kind of like a GPS. You put in a predestined address. You already know the final destination, but you still must travel the road to get there. You can't control the traffic or the other drivers. You can't control the weather. The car may break down along the way. Regardless, you continue driving. You drive according to the directions provided for the destination you know you're going to reach. God already knew where I was going. I just had to get there. My spirit was proclaiming and rejoicing because I was getting back on the predestined path written before I was formed.

That Wednesday something was different. Even though I spent a lot of time up north, driving in a snowstorm with eyes full of tears is a task for anyone. On this particular night, Holy Spirit had to have had the wheel because I could barely see. I just knew I had to get to someone's church. I saw a church with cars in the parking lot. I pulled in and parked. I contemplated not going in but something within me wouldn't let me leave. I walked in during bible study and sat in the back. To this day I can't tell you what was being taught. All I can remember is the peace that overshadowed me and calmed me instantly.

After service, I left before anyone could approach me. I got back in my truck and drove home. Once I reached home, immediately as I walked through the door, the confusion, anger, and frustration seemed to have waited for me. That night while lying in my bed, I prayed earnestly and sincerely for the first time in a while. Without knowing it, I applied Proverbs 16:3. I simply told God, "Lord I'm not sure what's going on, but something isn't right. Something is missing. If it be your will for me to stay and pursue my dreams, give me peace. But Lord if it's in your will for me to leave and move back down south please, give me a sign." That night I went to sleep and slept peacefully. Weeks would go by. By now I'm learning how to cope with the roller coaster of emotions I was dealing with. My life would change one Saturday afternoon as I sat in the basement looking at the snow outside my window. I received a phone call from my then 6-year-old daughter Kristina, who I'd just recently met a year prior. That's another story within itself. She began the conversation telling me about her grades and how well she was doing at school. I listened and encouraged her as any parent would, but a few minutes into the conversation she said something that would shift the very path of my life. Randomly she said, "Daddy, I love you!" I said "I love you too!" She said, "But, I want a daddy that's here all the time."

Luke 15:17 NIV
"When he came to his senses, he said,
'How many of my father's hired
servants have food to spare, and here I
am starving to death!"

After she spoke these words, my heart broke. For the first time I understood what the prodigal son felt when he came to himself. Some translations say he came to his senses.

It was at that precise moment I realized God heard my prayer and had spoken through my daughter. He knew the exact moment and the exact vessel to use. There's something about a daughter that a true father can't deny. I got off the phone with her and begin to cry because I knew what I had to do next. I had to leave everything I ever thought I wanted and worked for behind in order to have peace of mind. Initially I thought to myself, "So that's what the stress was about. God just wanted me to move back closer to home to be close to my children." Years later I would finally learn there was so much more to it.

    Leaving my friends and music behind was the hardest thing I'd ever done. I often wondered and worried, "What if they make it without me? What if when I leave, they get the big deal?" What if, what if, what if…? Needless to say, I was whole and torn at the same time.

    A few months after the call, I packed up and moved to Dallas, Texas. I'd drive 1,188 miles by myself with a U-Haul attached to my truck. The weight of the U-Haul would only allow me to drive 55 miles per hour. Thank God gas was cheap at the time. Many times, while on the trip I thought about turning around and going back to Detroit, but I had already seen myself completing the drive. Don't start until you've seen yourself finish.

What was it about that one Sunday morning that was different? What was I feeling inside? What happened to my confidence in my own abilities? Why did I suddenly start feeling out of place? What happened? Purpose happened. It's no coincidence that of all of the people outside of the music industry I was drawn to, I was drawn to 2 young ladies named Crystal and Shanell; Christians. They were true friends and sisters that didn't judge me but rather just unknowingly walked with me in the right direction by making sure they were in church on Sunday. When your life has been ordained by God, nothing happens by coincidence.

Psalm 37:23-24 KJV
The steps of a good man are ordered by
the Lord: and he delighteth in his way.
Though he fall, he shall not be utterly
cast down: for the Lord upholdeth him
with his hand.

He called me a "good man." Regardless of my mistakes. Regardless of my flaws. Regardless of my shortcomings, I'm a good man.

When you live life on purpose, not even accidents can keep you down.

Upon moving leaving my group and moving to Dallas, there were things that made it difficult after I returned down south. For a while I was talked about so bad because people felt as though I let them down. To a personal degree, I did let them down. I withdrew and treated them like they wouldn't understand. Nevertheless, I had to make a decision that was very unpopular.

Over the years I learned that lifting Jesus up meant often letting people down. I had to realize that His vision was much clearer than my dreams. Even when I fall, because my steps are ordered, He picks me up. When you live a life of purpose, not even accidents can keep you down. You never have to apologize for what you did on purpose. You did it with the intention of being successful.

Power Points of Purpose:

CHAPTER FOUR

MY WILL, I WILL. HIS WILL, HE WILL.

In the beginning God spoke. In the beginning God created. In the beginning God knew that we would be exactly where we are in life. From the foundation of the earth, God's preparations for us and gave us purpose. Freewill has been our fall. We as human beings don't always make the best choices. In Genesis 2 starting at verse 16, God told Adam (KJV), "Of every tree of the garden thou mayest freely eat: but the tree of the knowledge of good and evil, thou shalt not eat of it: for in the day that thou eatest thereof thou shalt surely die." Why plant the tree and then tell us not to touch it? Why make it accessible? Why even bring light to the tree?

God is a relational God. Just like any other relationship we encounter, we have both verbal and non-verbal rules, right? Like us, God wants to be chosen and selected and not just tolerated. By revealing the Tree of the Knowledge of good and evil, He (God) was giving man an opportunity to choose life over death. In order for man to decide, it was only fair that man have all of the information. God had given man complete dominion. With dominion comes power. With God giving power and dominion to Adam, it was only right for Adam to know exactly what he was responsible for. Look at it like this. If someone gives you 2 dogs to care for, wouldn't you like to know that character and mannerisms of the animals you're expected to care for? One is a playful and fun-loving dog. You have no problem with your children or anyone for that matter being around this dog. However, the other is playful, fun-loving, and may bite if played with or loved on. Is that information important? You've been warned of the consequences. What's your next move? Adam knew the consequences of what he was doing, and yet chose to forfeit a portion of his purpose in order to satisfy people and curiosity.

The Tree of the knowledge of good and evil, bore two different kind of fruit, good and evil. Meaning the tree was double-minded. The tree was unstable. The tree had no other purpose other than to confuse the people who partook of it. I imagine, it looked beautiful. The tree may have even towered over other trees just to bring more attention to itself. The tree offered a variety of flavors. While the other tree beside it only offered one flavor called Life. The tree of knowledge offered a great time. It offered more knowledge. It offered an opportunity that would create your own path instead of the path God laid out. It offered independence, freedom from God. It also offered fruit such as bitterness, anger, disobedience, murder, shame, nakedness, double-vision, and confusion. It offered spiritual death by separation. In the beginning Adam made a decision that would cost us our identity as God's children. Not that God doesn't know who we are but we as the people of God don't know who we are. When you don't know who you are, you will be whatever anyone else wants you to be. When you don't

*When you don't know who you are,
you will be whatever anyone else wants
you to be.
When you don't know whose you are,
you will give yourself to anyone who
will take you.*

know whose you are, you will give yourself to anyone who will take you. Feeling mistreated, misunderstood, and misplaced are common side effects from eating of the wrong tree.

Many of us right now today have noticed a longing for more. We've noticed that we have a desire to do something or be something that's against what we've always done. Sadly, what most of us will do is trust and depend on the validation and confirmation of people. Some will never seek the creator and lover of their souls in order to uncover the purpose that's already in them. A lot of people will continue working on jobs believing that their purpose is solely in their occupation. But not you! You're getting ready to uncover something really big.

The word Boulema (pronounced boo'-lay-mah) is a Greek word that means will, counsel, or purpose. Jesus said in John 6:38 (NIV) "For I have come down from heaven not to do my will but to do the will of Him who sent me." In the following verse Jesus, went further by telling the people what the will of the Father was. Jesus was identifying the purpose, plan, and reason He was sent to this earth. One thing I love about this verse is, Jesus didn't deny or even ignored the fact that He, Himself as flesh, had another plan, purpose, and reason. However, He denied what Jesus in the flesh may have wanted to do in order to be obedient to the will of His Father. He stuck to the plans that were drawn up for his existence. He lived out the purpose of His creation. He understood the reason He was assigned.

    Even when facing death, He reminded Himself who's will, who's purpose, and who's plan was important. As He was in the Garden of Gethsemane, Jesus begin to have second and third thoughts about following through with His purpose. He knew the amount of pain and torture He would endure. He knew the lies people would tell. He knew the betrayal He would face. He'd receive a kiss from the one who would turn on Him. He knew the tears that would fall from His mother's eyes as He would have to suffer while she looked on. He knew the people He protected, fed, saved from drowning, healed, and who's feet He'd washed would leave Him to take this burden alone. Knowing all of this, Jesus sought God not once, but three times (Luke 22:39-46) in an effort to change the will of God for His life. One thing that really impressed me about Jesus as He was battling between His will and the Father's will, Jesus never appeared broken, hurt, afraid, or vulnerable to his disciples. Only three of them were within a stone's throw while He prayed. Jesus, in His heart, knew that this moment was purely between Him and His Father. Had the disciples saw Jesus vulnerable, what would have become of their choices in the future when they would face adversity? How blessed are we that we've been allowed a preview of the soul of our Savior at the point of wanting to walk away from His purpose, but instead endured and followed through.

    Jesus made a choice. He said, "Nevertheless not my will, but thine be done." Shortly after submitting to the will of God, the bible says an Angel from Heaven appeared and strengthened Him. Some translations say an angel ministered to Him. The word minister means to help. Eve was created as a help-meet. Therefore, her responsibility was to minister to Adam as he would have the weight of the world on his shoulders. Much at this time, Jesus needed help and strength to complete the task set before Him. God didn't send the help until Jesus surrendered to the will of His Father. Help comes at the point of submission.

God will not leave you without strength to complete the mission He's commissioned you to complete. If its "my will" I will bear the responsibility and consequences for whatever I choose. If I choose "His Will" He will see to it that He who has begun a good work in me will carry it on to completion until the day of Christ Jesus. Philippians 1:6 (NIV). Jesus submitted His personal will for God's will. Submission is an act of humility. Humility is the fear of the Lord; its wages are riches and honor and life. Proverbs 22:4 (NIV). It takes humility to seek God, trust God, and obey God. Your purpose is to honor the will of God that He has for your life.

I don't know about you, but this blessed my soul completely. To know that my Lord and Savior, left Heaven on purpose with purpose. He didn't leave on accident. He wasn't kicked out. He left Heaven with a plan. He left Heaven for a reason. He left Heaven with a Boulema! He came to do the will of God on behalf of God's people! He loves me so much, He allowed Himself to feel my fears, my anxiety, my depression, my loneliness, my desire to quit, and my pains. But more than that, He loved me enough to reach past His pain and follow through with the reason, the plan, and the purpose in order to fulfill the will of the one who sent Him to die in my place. He loved me enough to allow me to see Him at the point of giving up, but even after not receiving an answer to abort the mission, He decided to finish the work.

Why is this important? It's important that you know you were created with a plan in mind. Although life has presented some tough times and some new ways, it's always best to seek direction from the One who sent you. It's always best to express your truest emotions and desires. Lastly, it always best to start what's already finished. Before Jesus gave up the ghost he spoke, "It is finished!"

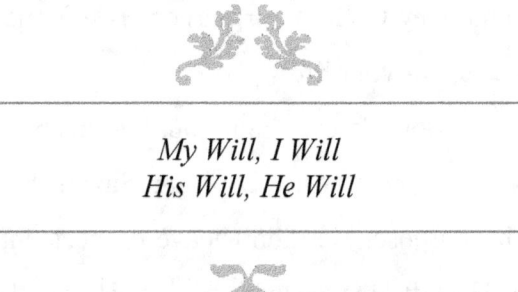

My Will, I Will
His Will, He Will

For I know the plans I have for you says the Lord, plans to prosper you and not harm you, plan to give you hope and a future. Jeremiah 29:11 (NIV). Your future looks amazingly bright.

Power Points of Purpose:

CHAPTER FIVE

BECAUSE

Sometimes our natural ability can get in the way of our true purpose.

God has given everyone the tools necessary to make it on the earth. We're all blessed with something that will finance our way through life. Many of us rely on education or some sort of training to make ends meet. Some of us are good with tools, some are good with numbers, some are even good with animals, but is that completely it? Is that all God created you to do? Or is this just a bridge or training ground for your ultimate purpose? Could God be withholding the clarity of your purpose, on purpose?

In the book of 1st Samuel, we find a young childless wife named Hannah. Hannah would become the mother of one of the most powerful prophets in the old testament. She wouldn't do this without complication or conflict. Samuel was a prophet whose purpose would define his birth. In fact, he was an answer to prayers prayed and a promise made. Samuel's mother was unable to conceive children. Verse 6 of 1st Samuel Chapter 1 states, "Because the Lord had closed Hannah's (Samuels mother) womb, her rival kept provoking her in order to irritate her." In the bible, it was common for a man to have more than one wife. Hannah shared a husband with another woman named Penninah who conceived regularly. Elkanah, their husband, would give Hannah double-portions of any sacrifice because her womb was closed, and he loved her.

Verse 6 starts off with the word "Because." Often when we speak, we use the word "Because" to introduce the explanation or give the reason for a certain decision or plan of action. Why are you reading? Because, I want knowledge. Why are you eating? Because, I'm hungry. We never use the word "Because" if asked who, what, when, or where. We only use "Because" after being asked, Why? The word "Because," indicates there is a reason why God closed Hannah's womb.

In this verse, God is identified as the closer and the architect of her unfruitful season. She was irritated and discouraged because she may not have understood why others who really didn't value carrying a child were so fruitful. Having a good strong husband who gave her everything she ever needed wasn't good enough for her. There was something missing.

For years Hannah was teased and humiliated by her husband's (Elkanah) other wife, Penninah. Even as Hannah would go to worship, her rival would make fun of her and remind her of what she was incapable of doing. It seems harsh that God would allow her to suffer like this. It seems unfair that someone, Penninah, who has everything, shows very little compassion for someone who deserves everything.

Obviously, Hannah and Elkanah were trying to conceive but were unsuccessful for years. I can only imagine Hannah's self-esteem was at the point of giving up. Many of us walking in purpose see so many others who seem to blow the opportunities we so badly want. We see people squander off millions of dollars on riotous living. We think to ourselves, if I had half of that, I'd do so many other things. In a lot of cases, I've talked to and counseled a lot of young ladies who've been unable to carry a child full term or at all. The hurt and the anger of unfairness that flows through their tears when they see and hear of people aborting, leaving, or even murdering children is unexplainable. Surely in their minds they are thinking, Why? Surely in their hearts they are asking God, Why not me?

Hannah wasn't a weak woman. In fact, she was very strong. Each year she faithfully traveled to the House of the Lord with her husband, his other wife, and all of their children. She sat and ate dinner with the very people who irritated and humiliated her. One year, after completing dinner at the House of the Lord, the bible says she begins to pray and weep bitterly. While she was in the House of the Lord, she was in the presence of the Man of God, Eli. She began to pray to the one responsible for closing her womb. She begins to pray to herself while she cried. Perhaps this is what the Lord was waiting on. Could God have been waiting on her to shift her focus from her desires to the purpose. The purpose of who she would carry in her womb. "Lord Almighty, if you will only look on your servant's misery and remember me, and not forget your servant but give her a son, then I will give him to the Lord for all the days of his life, and no razor will ever be used on his head." Hannah prayed to the giver of purpose. It was at this point that she realized that, my womb has been preserved. It was no longer about what others thought. It was no longer about how she'd been mistreated. It was about pleasing God. She submitted her womb and her seed back to the Lord even though there was no evidence of life.

In the eyes of the man of God, Eli, she looked and acted drunk. He had never seen a woman pray in the manner that Hannah was praying in. He began to rebuke her and accused her of being drunk. She responded, "Not so, my lord," I am a woman who is deeply troubled. I have not been drinking wine or beer; I was pouring out my soul to the Lord. Don't take your servant for a wicked woman; I have been praying here out of great anguish and grief."

This statement she made, "I was pouring out my SOUL." is monumental. This statement is the where the shift happened. Exactly what was she doing?

We are made up of Spirit, flesh, and our SOUL. Our Spirit will return back to God when our days on earth are done. Our spirit was given to us by God. Our spirit is God's image in us. Our spirit is our life-line to the Father. The flesh is the vessel that houses our spirit and our SOUL. Our SOUL is the seat of our emotions, thoughts, attitude, decisions, motives, and desires. When we meet our Savior face to face, it's our SOUL that will be judged. Our SOUL will either follow the desires of the Spirit or fulfill the desires of the flesh. In the decision-making process, we develop our character. Often when we are led by the flesh, we make impulse decisions that give immediate satisfaction. The complete opposite happens when we are led by the spirit. When we are led by the spirit, we think outside of our emotions and we make decisions that have more of a positive effect on where we're going. When we discover or gain a hunger for purpose, we often decide to please God over pleasing ourselves, knowing that please God ultimately takes beyond where we've ever dreamed.

In the previous verse, Hannah said, "I was pouring out my soul to the Lord." I was getting rid of the anguish and the grief. I was pouring out in order to be filled again. Only an empty vessel requires refilling. Hannah poured out her emotions, her thoughts, her attitude, her decisions, her motives, and her desires. In return, God filled her soul with purpose. Not only did she pour out of her soul, she then told God specifically what she wanted and made a vow to God. Lord, I'm submitting my will for yours. Give me a son and I will give Him back to you. A razor will not touch his head (Raised as a Nazarite). Give me a son to fulfill your desires, your plan, and your

Only an empty vessel requires refilling.

---

purpose. I no longer want a child just because I'm a woman. I want to be the vessel you use to bring forth a child that will shake up the nation for your Glory. Use my vessel Lord to produce the one you will use to bring order to your people.

After Hannah explained to Eli what she was doing, Eli, the Man of God, blessed her and came into agreement with what she asked. He had no idea that he came into agreement with her giving birth to the child who would one day replace him. After she left, her anguish and grief were gone. Here's where faith stepped in. After returning home, not out of obligation, not out of obedience, but Hannah made love to her husband on purpose! She believed that what she asked God for was already done. Faith without works is dead. Oh, I know it's a little humorous, but watch. She asked God for something. She poured out all of her bitterness, anger, anguish and grief. Even when she was falsely rebuked, she respectfully enlightened the Man of God of her actions. She then received his blessing. After submitting unto the Lord, she then submitted to her husband by faith. She did her part believing that God would do His.

After a course of time, meaning at an appointed time, Hannah became pregnant and gave birth to a son. She named him Samuel. After she weaned him, she remembered the promise she made unto the Lord. During the annual sacrifice, she took Samuel back to the Man of God, Eli. She reminded Eli. "I am the woman that stood by you here praying unto the Lord. This is what I was praying for. The Lord has answered my prayer which I asked of Him. I have given him back to the Lord. For as long as he lives, he shall belong to the Lord." After God blessed her with what she asked, she didn't forget the vow that she made. She honored her vow, even if it meant letting go of what she received. She realized that God's purpose for Samuel was the reason her womb was closed. Hannah had every opportunity to renege on her promise but because of purpose, she followed through.

Eli, blessed Elkanah and his wife Hannah. He said, "The Lord give thee seed of this woman for the loan which is lent to the Lord (KJV). He asked God to bless her with even more children because of the one she dedicated back to the Lord. She and Elkanah left Samuel with Eli. Samuel lived at the House of God where he served and helped the Man of God daily. Even though Eli had his own sons, neither of them had the purpose for which Samuel was created. The Lord visited Hannah and blessed her womb to carry and give birth to five more children, three sons, and two daughters. Hannah, I'm so happy for you. You waited and even sacrificed your relationship with your first child in order for him to fulfill the purpose that God had already placed over his life. Because of your offering to the Lord, your womb was blessed.

The most important revelation in this chapter is Hannah found her "Because." She realigned her motive when her reason for wanting a child was changed. When it became about giving Glory to God, God opened the womb. For a season, God closed Hannah's natural womb. She was unable to do what she was naturally created to do. Sometimes our natural ability can get in the way of our true purpose. When we are seeking supernatural purpose through a natural means, many times we can miss the mark. As stated earlier, God has equipped each of us with what we need to operate naturally. When we're seeking purpose from a Super-natural God, it may take removing our natural desires and focusing on the reason and motives of why we seek purpose.

Power Points of Purpose:

CHAPTER SIX

YOU'RE NOT BEHIND

Right now, I think it's important that we tackle a serious character that we've allowed to enter our souls. Anxiety. Truthfully, we have more in common with the people in the bible than we think. Hannah was grieved and anguished due to the constant pressure to produce.

Sarah in Genesis 16 also felt and experienced anxiety because she was old and had not yet begun a family of her own. Gideon, in Judges 6, felt fear and insecurity because the task he was called to take on was bigger than he was. Hosea was a preacher who was led to marry a prostitute. He was ready to give up on the marriage. Jonah was called to preach to people he didn't care for. Justified in his human nature, Jonah ran and decided not to preach because he wanted to see the people who oppressed his people get what they deserved. However, this wouldn't work out for him because he failed to realize that the people, he decided not to preach to were loved by God just as much as he was loved by God. When Jonah tried to run away from his purpose, he was stabilized in the belly of a fish.

Somewhere in each of these stories, we can identify or we know of others who can identify with these emotions.

The pressure we put on ourselves to be at a certain point in life by a certain time produces a level of anxiety and undue pressure. As people of the Most High God we know that God does everything at an appointed time. Meaning God sets everything in order according to purpose. Don't get me wrong, there's nothing wrong with having goals and a plan. In fact, we are instructed through the word of God to write the vision and make it plain (Habakkuk 2:2). We are encouraged to have a vision. Without a vision people perish right? What we can't forget in our search for purpose is the giver of the vision. We can't overlook the writer of the plan. Psalm 37:23 says, The steps of a good man are ordered by the Lord: and he delighteth in his way (KJV). Proverbs 16:3, Commit to the Lord whatever you do, and He will establish your plans (NIV). Proverbs 3:5-6 teaches us to, Trust in the Lord with ALL your heart and lean NOT on your own understanding; in all your ways submit to Him, and He will make your paths straight (NIV). These scriptures are encouraging us as followers and believers of God to follow and believe in God. They are telling us to be "God-Confident!" These scriptures are instructing us to not only write the vision but commit it and submit it to God before we try to establish it on our own.

In the last chapter, Hannah submitted her womb to the Lord. She submitted her child to the Lord. She spoke exactly what she wanted and told God what she would do with the child upon receiving him. When she submitted to the will of God, her anxiety, grief, anguish, and misery left her because now it's no longer in her hands. She's now fully relying on God (Isaiah 10:20-27). The world deals with anxiety, grief, depression and many other mental issues with prescriptions. As the people of God, our first line of defense should always be scripture. Scripture brings peace and a reminder of promises made. When I know that my steps are ordered by God, I trust that in His time and season (Ecclesiastes 3), He will bring to pass what He has promised. Later on, I will share with you how I know this works.

The world's way of dealing with issues is through prescriptions. The Kingdom of God's way is through Scripture.

Samuel had a purpose spoken over his life before he was conceived. In fact, it was his mother's acknowledgment of his purpose that allowed her womb to be opened. Once Samuel was weaned from his mother, he was taken to the House of God and given to the Man of God to serve in the temple. Elkanah and Hannah fulfilled their vow to God by dedicating their son to the work of God. Eli, the priest, received and took on the responsibility of raising and teaching Samuel. At this time, Eli had no idea he was raising and training the young man who would one day replace him as the spiritual leader of God's people.

Eli had 2 sons named Hophni and Phin'ehas. Eli hadn't raised his sons in the fear of the Lord, but yet he allowed them to be positioned in leadership over the people of God. Family tradition in this case afforded Hophni and Phin'ehas a seat at the table that they were not qualified to take. They had no respect for the things of God. They had no respect for the office. They were wicked.

1st Samuel 2:12-17 (NIV)

Eli's sons were scoundrels; they had no regard for the Lord.
Now it was the practice of the priests that whenever any of the people offered a sacrifice, the priest's servant would come with a three-pronged for in his hand while the meat was being boiled

and would plunge the fork into the pan or kettle or caldron or pot. Whatever the fork brought up the priest would take for himself. This is how they treated all the Israelites who came to Shiloh. But even before the fat was burned, the priest's servant would come and say to the person who was sacrificing, "Give the priest some meat to roast; he won't accept boiled meat from you, but only raw." If the person said to him, "Let the fat be burned first, an then take whatever you want," the servant would answer, "No, hand it over now; if you don't, I'll take it by force." This sin of the young men was very great in the Lord's sight, for they were treating the Lord's offering with contempt.

Verse 17 in KJV states:

Wherefore, the sin of the young men was very great before the Lord: for men abhorred the offering of the Lord.

Now we're beginning to see why Hannah's womb was saved. We're starting to see why God closed her womb until she recognized that the child she would carry would have an assignment that would shift the foundation of the world as they knew it. Eli never disciplined his sons. Eli allowed his sons to do as they pleased when it came to the people of God. Had Eli died without God making provisions, Hophni and Phin'ehas would be the overseers of the people of God. Hophni and

Phin'ehas has no respect for God. Neither did they have respect for the office their father held. All they saw were the benefits of being Eli's sons. Verse 17 says that the men of the Israel abhorred God's offering. People hated giving. They hated going to the temple. They hated being subject to disrespect and humiliation. They watched as their offering to God was pillaged over by those who had no respect for the God they were offering to. The young men were impatient. They didn't want to wait until the fat, God's portion, was reduced or melted way. They wanted it all. They wanted God's portion and the portion that God saved for them. They were greedy.

It didn't stop there. Eli was old, partially blind, and overweight. His sons took advantage of his disabilities. They would lay with the women that assembled at the door of the tabernacle of the congregation (v.22). The people of God would complain to Eli. He would speak to his sons, but he never removed them from their positions.

God never assigned these young men to the position they were in. It was Eli's job to protect the people of God. Even if that meant protecting them from His sons. Eli chose loyalty to his blood family over loyalty to his spiritual purpose. He chose to create a legacy through his family over allowing God to select for Himself, the man that would succeed him in the priesthood.

There are some families that are rich with ministry. Rich with revelation. Rich with the purpose of the Lord for the church. However, it is a dangerous thing to put the people of God in the hands of someone of your choosing and not God's calling.

My family is rich with preachers and pastors. For me, this was the very last thing I wanted to do. In fact, I tried to prove to God that I wasn't the one he wanted. Growing up I heard often, "You're going to preach, just like your dad!" My dad would always rebuke that person. He would say, "You let God do the calling and assigning!" He often told me, "If you can help it, don't do it!" My dad never pressured me to be like him. He never encouraged me to follow in his footsteps. Even though in his heart, he may have wanted me to, he never pressed the issue. I believe that he knew in his heart that I would one day take the mantle, but he relied on God to speak that into my life. I can imagine there were times that he and my mom may have lost hope in me due to my riotous living. I'm thankful that I was allowed the opportunity to hear God for myself. Each case is different; however, the warning is the same. Eli, was chosen by God to lead His people. His sons weren't.

The Call

As Samuel served and helped Eli before the Lord, He grew. It is believed that Samuel was 11 years old when the Lord called his name. One night as Samuel was asleep, a voice called out his name (v.3). Samuel believing that he was hearing Eli, got up and ran to Eli and said, "Here am I. You called me." Eli stated, "I didn't call you." The bible says that Samuel did not know the Lord. This is powerful right here. Although Samuel was born with a purpose to serve, lead, and prophecy, He did not know God. He's never heard the voice of God. Even while serving and working in the House of God, he did not know God. So being that Samuel didn't know God, there was no way for him to discern God's voice. God, in His infinite wisdom, knew that Samuel was used to taking instruction from and serving Eli. Samuel knew Eli's voice. God is using a familiar voice to get the attention of Samuel. When one's relationship with God doesn't exist or they're new to the faith, God will use a familiar voice in order to get a message to them. Some of the members at our church often say they hear my voice when they are about to make a decision that would cost them.

After Samuel returned back to bed, the voice of the Lord called him again. For a second time, Samuel, got up, ran to Eli, "Here I am, you called me?" "No son. I didn't call you." A third time, "Samuel!" Samuel, got up, ran to Eli, "Here I am, you called me?" By this time Eli realizes that God is calling Samuel. Eli, realized that God was raising up another prophet. Instead of answering Samuel himself, he told Samuel who was calling him and then gave Samuel the words (tools) to respond. At this moment Eli realized that Samuel's purpose was bigger than even he had imagined. Where he had placed legacy through his sons, God provided for Himself a ram in the bush. Even though this move of God wouldn't personally benefit Eli's family, it would personally and spiritually benefit the people of God. Eli didn't stand in the way of Samuel's purpose. In fact, he helped usher Samuel into his purpose even if it meant his desires for legacy would be rejected. Eli had a choice when it came to his sons. It was his lack of direction and correction that caused the mantle to be removed from his house.

Samuel answered the voice of the Lord. The message he received would test his loyalty and his purpose. Even at 11 years old, Samuel was faced with living out his purpose to the glory of God or retracting from his purpose to save a personal relationship. Under pressure from Eli, Samuel revealed the truth of the message from God about Eli. The message spoke of the future of Eli's family for his inconsistencies as a leader. Samuel chose to speak what God spoke regardless of the outcome of his relationship with the man who raised him as a servant of God.

Samuel served and worked for years. Even though he didn't know the Lord in the beginning, God still had a purpose and plan already drawn out for him. Even while Eli prepared for his sons to take the office, not even he as high priest could take from Samuel what was rightfully and purposefully for him. When God promotes, He promotes with purpose. In fact, it's the purpose that provides the promotion. No one can take what

It's the purpose that provides the Promotion.

God has promised you. Even though it may seem like your true purpose is avoiding you, just know that you're not behind. Everything God does, He does in decency and in order. He does what He does at appointed times. Let's just say, by appointment only. Before you go to the doctor, chances are you have an appointed time to see him/her. Even when you're early, your time is set. The best thing you can do is just be available when your name is called.

Power Points of Purpose:

CHAPTER SEVEN

RELAY

(PASS THE BATON)

In high school I ran track. I wasn't the fastest, neither was I the slowest. I couldn't outrun you in a hundred-meter dash, but I'd probably outlast you in a 400-meter dash. Some people actually get stronger, the longer they run. The first time I ran the 400, I was actually deceived by my coach into running it. We were sitting on the bus right before a practice meet. Coach really didn't know the type of runners he had. Of course, he knew the fastest guys and the guys who could run the long distance. I was neither of those. Like many others, I joined the track team to keep from participating in off-season football workouts. On this particular day, Coach was going over the roster and making sure he had someone participating in every race. He realized that he didn't have a runner for the 400. So, he unenthusiastically said, "Does anyone want to run the 400?" This was my first time ever running track, so I ignorantly ask, "Coach, What's the 400?" To which he truthfully and deceptively replied, "Oh, it's JUST one time around the track."

Me thinking, "That's all? Coach, I got it!" I should've taken notice that absolutely NO ONE else volunteered to run this race.

The time would come for my race. As I'm walking to the track, Coach begins to tell me of the rules of the run. "You're in lane 7. It just seems like you're far ahead but you're not. The guys in lane 1 and 2 seem like they are far behind, but they're not. He said, "Sprint the curve and coast the straight away. When you get around the first curve. As they begin to catch up don't worry about them. Keep your pace. Save your energy for the final curve. The last 220 meters at the top of the curve, give it everything you've got." Sounds simple. Runners to your mark, get set, POW! The gun goes off. I'm sprinting as fast as I can. I'm blowing past my competition in lanes 9 and 10. Feeling like oh this is simple. Coming out of the curve, I was the leader. But somewhere along the first straight away, the others seem to be coasting at full speed, so I exerted more energy trying to keep my lead. As we approached the final 220, I could hear the coach screaming, "Now! Turn it on!" What he didn't realize was that I was already turned on in the process of turning it off. My legs were locking, buttocks screaming, lungs collapsing, and head spinning. You name it, I was feeling it.

As I watched all those that I ran past in the beginning, now blow past me in the final stretch, all I could do was congratulate them as they ran by. At the 30-meter mark, I had the track all to myself as the other runners had completed the race. I was dead last. I literally stumbled across the finish line.

Embarrassed and ready to regurgitate, I took my walk of shame. My coach ran towards me with excitement, holding the stopwatch. I didn't know how to react because his emotional outburst compared to my last-place finish that I'd just blessed the track with, just didn't add up. He looked at me and said, "Look at that time! You've never run that race before. You under-estimated it." Correction Coach, you under-sold it! "You're 14 and you just ran the 400 in :58 seconds," he said. "You've never been trained on it. With training, you'll be able to beat all those guys the next time you run it." Me personally, all I heard was "NEXT TIME." I'm thinking to myself "NEXT TIME?" The joke was on him, so I thought. He then told me, "You'll be running the anchor on the 400-meter relay at some point this year."

I took on a race that seemed easy. I under-estimated the distance. I started off too fast and spent too much energy trying to stay with the pack that was already trained and experienced. What I didn't realize was my coach was more concerned about the time and how I ran the race than he was the last-place finish. He saw a young man who was willing to try something and complete it even though he had no idea what he was doing. He saw a young man, who in spite of getting passed over and laughed at, finished the race. He saw a young man who stepped up when others stepped back. It was then, he knew my purpose on his team. This one won't quit. This one will try. This one will take a chance. As the season progressed, I had to learn how to run the race.

Just like he spoke earlier in the season, I would go on to be the anchor on the mile relay within the next couple of years. I'd grown comfortable with starting and finishing the race myself. However, becoming a part of a relay team required me to learn how to take and give the baton while not losing position. I had to learn how to run the race I was given, before trying to increase my load.

Running a relay requires a team effort. Everyone is accountable for their leg. Everyone has the responsibility of passing off the baton within a certain area in order to give the next man up the best opportunity to help the team win. While running an actual relay, the person carrying the baton is responsible for placing the baton in the hand of the person who will proceed in the race. The person receiving the baton is encouraged not to look back but to make sure their hand is available. The person receiving the baton is instructed to look forward and believe the person giving them the baton will get it to them at the right time. Even while waiting to receive the handoff, the runner in position to receive the handoff must not outrun the person giving the handoff. Timing (appointed) and position (posture) are crucial. If the handoff is missed or given out of the appropriate lane assigned, the entire team is disqualified from the race.

What we truly lack in the Body of Christ today is a relay team. The spirit of competition has outlasted the spirit of purpose. Many are falling by the away having never passed or received the baton. What we're seeing now is a lot of sprinters who lack the discipline and the stamina to wait for the baton and to pace themselves when their time has come to run the race. We're sprinting when we should be at a steady pace. We're trending when we should be changing.

When you know your purpose, it's the timing you're concerned about, not the person in the other lane who seems to be ahead of you. The appointed time; Am I where I'm supposed to be when I need to be there? When you know your purpose, you run your race. Some of us are missing the mark because those who went before us view us as competition instead of an extension. How can you run a relay if you left before the baton was passed? If it was never passed to you, what do you have to pass to anyone else? This message is for the giver and the receiver of the race. The giver was once the receiver. When it's time to give, give without worry. When it's time to receive, be where you're assigned to be so that the giver has full confidence that you can continue the pace without abandoning the race.

Ecclesiastes 9:11 says:

I have seen something else under the sun: The race is not to the swift or the battle to the strong, nor does food come to the wise or wealth to the brilliant or favor to the learned; but time and chance happen to them all.

This scripture is saying, just because one is fast, just because one is strong, just because one is educated, just because one is wise, doesn't mean they will be purposed in the area of their speed, strength, or wisdom. It's saying the purpose isn't always built around what you do well on your own. But an appointed time and an opportunity happens to and for everyone. It's saying don't disqualify yourself because you're not trained or as experienced as others. Don't walk away in shame because you seem to be in last place. Don't get discouraged because you see someone else in a position you've unknowingly been in training for. When God is the giver of purpose, the odds will always seem to be stacked against you.

    Eli received word from young Samuel by way of the voice of God, that his season as priest would come to a horrible end. Although Eli received this unfavorable prophecy, he wasn't a stumbling block to Samuel. Eli realized that God's plan would come to pass with or without his approval. Eli knew the baton, the mantle, the purpose was being fulfilled and that his leg of the race was coming to an end. Eli and his sons would die tragic deaths due to their lack of accountability, disrespect, and arrogance. Samuel would then become the Prophet over Israel who would lead Israel under the reign of 2 of the most popular kings in the Old Testament, King Saul and King David.

Power Points of Purpose:

CHAPTER EIGHT

UNINVITED

The Prophet Samuel would go on to lead a life that would put him in very uncomfortable positions. At God's command, he would find, anoint, appoint, and disappoint the King that would rule the people of God. He would be the Ambassador of God. His prophetic presence wasn't received by the people as eagerly as we see prophets being received today. In fact, when Samuel entered a city, people feared his presence (1st Samuel 12:19-21). When Samuel spoke, the very things he spoke would soon come to pass whether good or bad. Can you imagine, the very purpose you've been given is to be God's mouthpiece. You have the assignment to speak everything God says regardless of how it makes people feel. An assignment like that could conflict with someone who wants to be liked, cheered, and loved by everyone. Wait, we do have people like that in this day and age. Samuel couldn't afford to compromise the Word of the Lord, and neither can we.

The children of Israel begin to cry out for a physical king. They complained to Samuel about not having a king.

They wanted to be like other nations. God took it as a personal rejection and spoke to Samuel and instructed Samuel to anoint and appoint Saul as King of Israel (1st Samuel 10). Even though he knew it wouldn't end well for Israel, Samuel was obedient. As time would have it, King Saul would rebel and lose his position as King because he began following the will of God's people over the will of God. God would then speak to Samuel about replacing King Saul with another man of God's choosing. Samuel found it difficult because he knew that King Saul would become enraged if he knew that he was being replaced. Not only that, Samuel and Saul had formed a personal relationship over the years. King Saul begin his journey in obedience, somewhere he lost sight of his purpose and started making decisions without consulting the Man of God. Samuel had to choose his purpose and obedience to God over his personal relationship with Saul.

In life, we are faced with crossroads. Many of us are faced with allowing relationships to fizzle. When God has purposed your life, there are simply some individuals who are not written in the next chapter of your life. Many of us struggle with allowing a season to come to an end. How often do we prove ourselves more loyal to our friends than we do to our God? Samuel himself was purposed to replace Eli. Samuel sat under Eli and came to know the Lord under Eli's covering. He,

Samuel, is now responsible for anointing and appointing another king to replace King Saul, his friend.

With the calling comes responsibility, loyalty, and obedience. I can imagine many people may have wanted the title Chief Prophet, but how many could actually follow through with what God spoke. Once purpose has been identified, you have the responsibility of living up to the calling. Loyalty to the one who purposed you is the only way to guarantee you'll

Remember who formed you.
Remember who anointed you.
Remember who appointed you.

complete the task. Finally, obedience is your only security. Often times obedience will isolate you from others you've formed a relationship with. The reason you were created outweighs any level of relationship you could form while here on earth. This doesn't mean treat people as if they don't matter, in fact, the people are all that matter. What this is saying is, remember who formed you. Remember who anointed you. Remember who appointed you.

God is Sovereign. Anytime we choose to deviate away from His plan, using His tools, His people, His prosperity, His Grace, His mercy, or His kindness we run the risk of being disappointed. King Saul continued to work even after God's spirit had departed from him (1 Samuel 16:14). Unbeknownst to him, God had already replaced Saul in spirit, but not in flesh with an overlooked shepherd boy named David.

In the beginning of 1 Samuel 16, we find Samuel mourning the rejection of Saul. God spoke, "How long will you mourn for Saul, since I have rejected him as king over Israel? It was time for Samuel to move on to the next phase of his purpose. As you walk in your purpose, you will experience ups and downs. You'll experience rejection and isolation. The question will one day ring in your spirit, "How long will you mourn?

Fill your horn with oil and be on your way. I AM sending you!" Samuel was sent to Jesse in Bethlehem to anoint and appoint the next King of Israel. Upon reaching the city, people were in fear. Samuel announced that he'd come to sacrifice and have dinner. He then invited Jesse and Jesse's sons to the feast. Jesse, brought all of the sons he thought should be at the dinner. He overlooked the youngest. Maybe he felt as though David wasn't ready. Jesse could've just made a parental decision and assumed that this wasn't the kind of setting for David. More than likely, Jesse meant no harm by not including David. After all, he had 7 older sons that were strong, handsome, and ready to take on the world.

Before they sat to eat, Prophet Samuel took notice of the physical presence and stature of the oldest, Eliab. "Surely, the Lord's anointed stands before the Lord," Samuel said. The Lord spoke to Samuel at that moment and told him, "Take no thought of the man's appearance. Man looks on the outer appearance but God looks at the heart." Samuel, the Man of God, believed he knew the heart of God and attempted to select a King that God had not chosen. It's possible that Samuel considered his first encounter with King Saul. Saul too was a strong and handsome young man. What this tells me is that when you are walking in purpose, don't get used to a pattern. God is not predictable. "For my thoughts are not your thoughts, neither are your ways my ways," declares the Lord (Isaiah 55:8).

Even as a Man of God with years of relational experience with God, Samuel almost missed the mark by trying to see with his physical eyes. Samuel poured the oil on Jesse's first seven sons. God hadn't selected either of them. I begin to wonder, "Why, God? Why not just tell Samuel who you were looking for? I'm sure these young men may have been embarrassed after being rejected in front of family." The answer to this question leads me right back to purpose. Holy

Spirit whispered to me, "God knew beforehand who He sent Samuel to locate. However, Samuel didn't ask God who he was going to see. Samuel assumed by looking at the physical attributes of the sons, that God had selected based on appearance. But what Samuel didn't know is that the one that had been selected to carry on as King, would be one that most would consider the least qualified. Also, a lot of times we learn best by seeing what not to do." The oil that Samuel poured on the others didn't activate because the oil was designated for David. David was being groomed for an assignment by being overlooked by natural eyes.

After seven no's, Samuel asked, "Do you have another son? To this Jesse replied, "Yes, but he's the youngest. He's out shepherding the sheep." "We will not sit down to eat until I see him." Jesse sent for David and David came just as he was. He smelled like sheep. He was dirty. He was sweaty. But the bible indicates, he was handsome, fine appearance, healthy, and glowing. Then the Lord spoke to Samuel, "Rise, this is the one." Samuel took the horn of oil and anointed David in the presence of his brothers. The Spirit of the Lord came powerfully upon David (1 Samuel 16:13). David was anointed, but he had not yet been appointed. Samuel never disclosed why he was anointing any of Jesse's sons. The assignment wasn't revealed because the assignment wasn't to take place until an appointed time. After he was anointed, he was sent back into the field to continue his work as the shepherd of the sheep. Can you imagine the conversation once he returned back with oil dripping from his clothes? I can truly see his servants asking, what happened to you? "The Prophet Samuel is in town. Apparently, he's looking for someone. I'm not exactly sure what, but he poured oil on me. When he did, something

David was anointed, but he had not yet been appointed.

happened! My dad was there as well as my older brothers. They witnessed it. I'm not sure if they felt what I felt, but something happened."

Now let's dissect this and see how it applies to you. Let me encourage you first. You're being uninvited isn't a reason to be angry or bitter. Most of us who feel we've been overlooked tend to take it upon ourselves to be seen. When this happens, we pre-expose ourselves because the motive in wanting to be seen leads us away from God's will and into our own will. Samuel anointed seven other people. Because the purpose and position were designated for David, no one could sit in the seat. In fact, everything was delayed until David entered the room. It was a dinner in his honor, and he was the only uninvited guest. What does this say? This says, what God has for you is yours. You don't have to worry about anyone taking your purpose.

David's father knew exactly where he was when the Prophet summoned for him. He was in position. He was where he was supposed to be. He was working and tending his father's flock. He was behind the scenes doing the dirty work. He may have witnessed his brothers dressed and on their way to the party. He may have even seen the Prophet come to Bethlehem. If he didn't see it, I'm sure he heard about it. But what did he do? He stayed with his father's flock because it was what he was assigned to do at that time. I'm coming to realize that God likes to make an entrance.

David was the least and the last. He had the least amount of time to prepare HIMSELF. He didn't have an opportunity to clean himself up before he answered the call. He had to move into position when he was called upon. God uses whomever He chooses to use. When you are in position, you don't have to look for purpose. Purpose will find you. Purpose will call you by name.

Power Points of Purpose:

CHAPTER NINE

ANOINTED FOR THIS

Today we see the term anointed used so loosely in the Body of Christ. We hear or see talent and instantly a person is tagged anointed or "oily." The Hebrew word for anoint is "mashach (maw-shakh)." It means divine election or consecrated, solemn setting apart to an office. When one is anointed, they are anointed for a purpose, an assignment, a plan, a reason and a season. Having a skill does not qualify as being anointed if that skill doesn't have purpose. The purpose is the reason for the skill being given. As long as the person follows God's will for them, the anointing rest upon them. This is evident in how the Spirit of the Lord left Saul once Saul acted outside of God's purpose. The purpose is the "why" to having the skill. When David was anointed by Samuel, all of his skills became anointed as well. His skill set as a shepherd has now been divinely elected and consecrated. His ability to play the harp has been consecrated. The velocity and accuracy with his slingshot have been solemnly set apart. Even his bare hands as a fighter of lions and bears have been strengthened with power.

When you are anointed God doesn't just anoint what you do well. He anoints everything you touch. Have you ever touched something after you've put oil on your hand? Ever tried to scrub an oil stain off the parking lot? Ever tried to grip something with oily hands? People who have been anointed are anointed to carry and not grip. In other words, you realize you're just a vehicle to transport what you've been given the opportunity to carry. When you carry, you walk with more precaution because you don't want to run the risk of dropping what you're carrying. When you grip something with oily hands, there's a good chance that it will slip through your hands.

There's a difference in being gifted and talented. Many have been called gifted in an area where they're talented. There's absolutely nothing wrong with being talented. However, David's talent as a harp player didn't become gifted until he was anointed, and his skill now has purpose.

What does anointing mean again? Divine election, consecrated, solemnly set apart to an office. The purpose was to first, get him in King Saul's presence and then drive unclean spirits away. His playing the harp was his initial introduction to the king. It got him in the door. His gift made room for him. When your skillset or talent is operating with divine election, your gift will make room for you. A skillset or talent with the anointing (divine election, consecrated, solemnly set apart to an office) is a gift. Without the anointing, it's a talent in search of purpose. How many of us have laid aside the purpose of our talent for a few dollars? How many of us have stopped at the king's chamber and gotten comfortable with the king's ransom, not realizing this was just an introduction to where you would one day reign? God gives talent on purpose. God's purpose always comes with a plan. The thing about God's plan is it's not openly accessible. The only way to uncover God's plan is to live within His will. He said in Jeremiah 29:11, For I know THE plans I have for you. Not "A" plan, but "THE" plan. Meaning it's specific. It's yours. His plan may not be unfolded in its entirety. God operates in this fashion as a way of keeping our faith strong and flexible, as well as keeping the enemy guessing. God gives us the portion of our purpose that we can handle in the season we're in. He won't put no more on you than you can bear.

It's the purpose that allows you to walk in the Anointing.

The purpose and the anointing allow the talent to operate as a gift that is being purposefully used. Many people with talent never get discovered because they continue trying to use their talent outside of its purpose. People get paid every day to forget their purpose.

David, although anointed, still had to wait to serve until he was appointed. Even though he was selected by God to be the successor to King Saul, there was still a lot he had to learn. King Saul was handed the Kingdom. He didn't have to go through any proper training. His stature and his looks made it easier for the people to accept him as king. Without any effort of his own, he was granted the throne. David, on the other hand, was being groomed as a protector, a fighter, a leader, a lover of those things that couldn't fight for themselves, and a psalmist (he had a way with words-skilled musician). His training ground was the daily life as a shepherd boy. How amazing is our God to have the ability to take the least and the last and position them to do the most?

The day would come for David to make his introduction to the entire army of Israel. I told you God likes to make an entrance. Again, David was where he needed to be in order to receive instruction. He was with his father's sheep when he was instructed to go and check on his brothers who were on the frontline of the war between the Israelites and the Philistines.

In obedience, he took sorts of cheeses among other things and set off to do what his father had instructed him to do. This was nothing out of the norm. However, our ways are not God's ways. As David approached, he heard the champion of the Philistines, Goliath, cursing the Almighty God of Israel. He saw the Armies of Israel carrying on the characteristics as the King of Israel. They were afraid. David burned with anger due to the disrespect that was being hurled at his God. People within the army wanted David to take on the fight and they began to tell him what the King was willing to give to anyone who would fight Goliath and win. Even though the King's financial package was a good addition, David's motive was to defend the name of the Lord. David's motive was for the Kingdom of God. Matthew 6:33 says "Seek ye first the Kingdom of God and it's righteousness and all of these things will be added." The people put an emphasis on "these things" but David's motive was to slay the very person who disrespected God and God's people.

Jesse sent David for one thing, however, along the way God revealed the true purpose of David's journey. Let's look at the parallel of David's initial anointing and now David's introduction to being appointed. Seven people went before David before he was anointed as future king. They were all given the opportunity first, but the anointing wasn't theirs to carry. It was his all along. Again, he's away minding his father's sheep and war breaks out. He's called and sent with one agenda in mind, but upon arriving, not just seven people were there before him, but thousands were presented with the opportunity, but this was David's fight.

Here's the point:

Any time people are operating in a position that requires divine election and they've not been divinely elected; the weight of the position will weigh them down. Jesus said in John 10:12-13 **The hired hand is not the shepherd and does not own the sheep. So, when he sees the wolf coming, he abandons the sheep and runs away. Then the wolf attacks the flock and scatters it. 13. The man runs away because he is a hired hand and cares nothing for the sheep.**

Many people are being hurt following charismatic and trendy characteristics that look like a king, walk like a king, talk like a king, and even acts like a king. Some have even been groomed to succeed the current king. But the question is, "Did God divinely elect (anoint them as) the king? The purpose comes with an anointing (divine election). The appointing comes with a fight. When you're the only one appointed to the position, you're the only one anointed for the fight. Yes, you may have thousands around you watching and cheering you on, but you know yourself that you can't do it without God. People will offer you tangible gifts and monetary gain and "these things" are good, however, your motive should be to fight because it's your fight and not because you stand to gain financially. The God you serve anointed and appointed you, He is faithful to provide all of your needs.

As David would go on to fight Goliath. King Saul offered his battle gear. David considered wearing the kings war clothes but found Saul's clothing too big and too heavy for him. So, David chose to fight with what he knew best. He chose to fight a giant, *the introduction to his purpose, his introduction to the world*, with a sling and five rocks. David realized that the size of my opponent shouldn't scare me into using unfamiliar weapons. David realized, if it's my fight, I have to use the weapons I'm familiar with. God will not bring me a battle He's not equipped me for. Even though his weapons may have seemed small for such a big job, David used a principle of spiritual warfare before it was actually written: 2 Corinthian 10:3-4 (KJV), **For though we walk in the flesh, we do not war after the flesh: For the weapons of our warfare are not carnal, but mighty through God to the pulling down of strongholds;**

David realized the same power he felt when he was anointed by Samuel, is the same power that he's operating with right now. He's being driven by purpose. He didn't pick this fight, this fight picked him. David learned early that he couldn't go into a battle with a giant using weapons fit for a king. He had not yet arrived at the season of being king. He had to fight with the wisdom and the spiritual authority of a shepherd. Goliath mocked David and truly underestimated him because of his stature, his age, his lack of war gear, and inexperience. Because David was anointed (divinely elected) everything he touched carried the anointing as well. And with one smooth stone, David slew Goliath.

David was the only person who could've won in this fashion. It was his fight. It was his purpose. He was divinely selected for the assignment. When you find yourself in a season where you're facing a giant and you have more spectators than helpers, don't get offended at the spectators. Don't bash them subliminally on social media. Social media would encourage

When you're the only one appointed to the position, you're the only one anointed for the fight.

you to pay attention to those who don't help, but Kingdom Media would say, it wasn't their fight! You were anointed (divinely elected, consecrated, solemnly set apart for the office) to finish the job.

There was an incident at our church one night during revival. People were coming down for prayer. Many preachers were in attendance sprinkled throughout the congregation. Suddenly as I prayed over people, a young lady began to manifest an unclean spirit. Within a few seconds another woman, in the back of the church exposed her breast and begin rolling around on the floor. Many of the members without thought jumped into action. Through the power of Holy Spirit, we were victorious in helping these ladies get delivered. The next day, I found myself offended. I called my dad, (who's also a Pastor), to vent my frustrations at how most of the other ministers there didn't offer to assist. I went on to say how they just watched, did nothing to help us in warfare. At that time my dad corrected me. He simply stated, be careful in what you're saying. You had members that jumped in without warning to assist in deliverance. This wasn't everyone's battle, and neither is everyone assigned to handle what happened." He said, "Instead, of being angry, be thankful that no one acted like they were more prepared than they were. Be thankful that God's power prevailed." "Don't look down on a person because they're assignment is different than yours. There are somethings you don't do well, neither are you assigned to do that they are assigned to do. Stay humble and know, you were just the vessel that God used at that moment." Yes, my father rebuked me, and I received it. My perspective on ministry changed. My perspective on what it meant to be anointed (divinely elected) changed. We are all a part of one body. Each of us has been divinely selected to carry out a purpose. Like King David, no one has the ability to complete your assignment for you, but you.

Power Points of Purpose:

_____
_____
_____
_____
_____
_____
_____
_____
_____
_____
_____
_____
_____
_____
_____

CHAPTER TEN

TRANSITIONAL PHASE

The last few chapters have been centered around the lives of Hannah, Samuel, Eli, and David. I want to continue in the life and progression of another David. His name is David Roberson.

One thing I've learned over the last few years of my life is that my life is like a book in the bible. My life may be the only book someone may ever read. What was revealed to me is that the Apostles and Prophets taught through revelation and experience. They also preached from scripts which became a part of Holy Book we now live out. Their lives were scripture and they didn't know it. The same principle applies today. Our lives are scripture for someone watching and reading what we do.

When purpose found me, I wasn't trying to be found. I had no idea that everything I got involved with would lead me to where I am now. From the previous chapters, you saw where I made a choice to leave Michigan and move back down south in order to be closer to my children. You saw that God used my daughter to start the process of being re-locating. Just like King David. Jesse sent him to check on his brothers, but God sent him to deliver a nation.

I grew up with both parents in my home. I have a loving mother and an honorable father. So needless to say, I was raised right as the old folk would say. I had no reason, other than being rebellious, to go down the path I chose. At one point in my life, I was chasing a dream. I gambled my future as a father and a husband in an effort to become something because I had the talent or skillset to do it. Upon returning back to the south from the north, I found myself dealing with depression. I felt as though I had failed at everything. I felt like I was an embarrassment to the family due to the choices I made. No one ever made me feel this way. It was all a battle taking place in my mind. I'd play video games and drink myself to sleep in order to quiet the condemnation taking place in my mind. I knew God had heard me. I knew I was obedient in walking away from the very things I lived for. I felt as if, I'd lost everything even though I had nothing. I was too arrogant to listen or take advice from anyone who hadn't experienced what I'd experienced. Here I am a 25-year-old college drop out with 2 children 6 weeks apart. The only thing I had, so I thought, was my music and now I'm struggling trying to hold on to that.

My music was supposed to get me out of this rut. My music was the reason I left school. My music was the reason I left the south. My music was the avenue that would one day take care of my family. My music would solve all of my problems. It took years for me to realize that there are things that you may do well, however these things can potentially become the stumbling blocks that keep you from your purpose. Often, we get caught in transition. We never pass the baton.

I was so down in my spirit because I felt like God had abandoned me. One Wednesday morning I decided I needed to go to someone's church. Sounds familiar. I got off work and begin driving up Forest Lane heading to my apartment. I'd pretty much talked myself out of going to church on the commute home. I figured; this is how I ended up here. Why would I repeat this process? As I drove down Forest Lane, I tried to ignore the voice in my head that continued to urge me to turn right. Go to this church tonight. I was so convicted in my spirit to where I was uneasy and afraid to go home. I turned in to Greater Cornerstone Baptist Church, Pastor David. Ironically, another David. I went into the service that was already in progress. The choir was singing, and the musicians were locked. Locked as in sounding good. I couldn't believe this was just a Wednesday night service. The service was full of energy. Pastor spoke a word that night that spoke right to my spirit.

"God has not forgotten about you! He knows exactly where you were, where you are and where you're going." Needless to say, my spirit man calmed way down. I felt a familiar peace just knowing that God cared enough about me to send me to a random church and speak directly to me through someone I'd never seen.

I'd follow up that visit a few months later, again on a Wednesday night. On this particular Wednesday, the choir was singing again, and the musicians were locked. This is my favorite part. I grew up in church. I'd always loved good church music. Nothing like it on earth. I looked up in the choir stand and came eye to eye with a young man singing in the tenor section. I thought to myself, "You've got to be kidding me. This can't be, can it? Is that Danny?" Danny was a guy that I sang with years ago in college in Magnolia, Arkansas. He'd moved to Dallas long before I and the other guys moved to Detroit. I'm completely blown away now. After service, I waited around and sure enough, it's Danny. Danny would go on to introduce me to others at the church. I'd start attending choir rehearsals and bible study regularly. I was afraid to make the commitment to church because I "knew" how church was. I was just arrogant. Not only that, I was still trying to accomplish my dream with music. I'd started a record label with friends and even put out an R&B single shortly after I starting to attend church.

One Sunday, I decided to go. I got there a little late so there weren't any seats available towards the back. The usher ushered me down the right side to the second-row right by the drum set. After Pastor David preached, the invitation was given. I'd been heavily considering joining the church for a while, I'd never sat under another Pastor aside from my dad. Dad was untouchable. Not only that, I didn't want to start going and not have time to pursue my dreams. Excuses. Somehow, I struck up the nerve and walked down the aisle and united with the church. Immediately after joining, I became a part of the music ministry. "Maybe this is all God wanted," I thought. I became more and more involved at the church. I was changing. What was known about me before I was formed is now beginning to unfold.

I would continue growing each week. I'd attend the men's fellowship on Mondays, Bible Study on Wednesday, choir rehearsal on Thursday, and two services on Sunday. I was beginning to find my way back home. It didn't take much time to make my mark as a singer and a writer. What I realized as I grew was that I hadn't lost the desire to perform. The validation of the people was rooted very deeply within me. Yes, I'm growing into my purpose, but the influence of people still weighed heavy on my decisions. Not only did I make a physical transition, but I'd also soon be faced with a complete spiritual makeover.

The more I attended service the more I became convicted in my spirit about the direction I was still attempting to take outside of service. Of course, I knew the church lingo. I knew how to act churchy, speak churchy, even sing churchy, but my heart was in a war. One would think that all of the sacrifices I'd made would suffice, but I knew there was more. It's crazy when you have an appetite or a desire for something, but you just can't quite put a finger on it. Trust me, I was hungry. I found myself entering a phase where attending church was becoming equally as important to me as attending the club or any other social gathering. I found myself looking in the mirror saying, "Who are you?" Purpose would answer back, "I know you, but do you know you?"

Power Points of Purpose:

CHAPTER ELEVEN

UGLY PHASE

My parents still have photo albums. Each time I go to see my parents, I see old pictures on the wall in the garage and in photo albums. For my young readers, back in the day we had actual cameras that printed out the pictures right then. It was called a Polaroid Instant Camera. If you didn't have an instant camera, you may have had a box camera or some sort of camera you would have to extract the film from and take to the photo shop (the actual photo shop) and have the film developed. These photo albums, our parents still have, hold a lot of history. Everything from baby pictures, toddler years, teenage years, and even some from our adult years. In looking at these pics, one thing I notice about all of us is that we went through an ugly stage. Let me say I'm sorry to my sisters Teresa and Danielle. Yeah, y'all went through it too.

What we call the ugly stage is the stage in our physical lives when our bodies are changing and developing. I had a nose I hadn't quite grown in to, arms that were a few years older than me, and knees that hurt daily due to growing too fast in my upper body. No one wanted to call me their boyfriend at this stage. Many judged me because they saw me in the process of becoming the man I was growing to be. Not everyone can appreciate your ugly stage in life. Only a person that has been through a few ugly stages themselves can understand the process.

As you grow in Christ and your purpose begins to find you, you will go through a stage in your life where it seems like nothing is working. You'll go through years in your life where everyone who celebrated you, will quietly disappear. Worry will begin to rear its ugly head. Philippians 4:6 states, "Don't worry about anything, instead, pray about everything. Tell God what you need, and thank Him for all He has done." If what you're going through is part of the process of purpose, worrying won't cancel the process, but it could slow the process. When you've committed to following Christ everything you experience is absolutely necessary and vital for your growth in the area of your faith in God. You may not like His methods, but God wants to show you that He's trustworthy. The Sovereign Almighty God is giving you the opportunity to trust Him with your life. He's giving you the opportunity to fulfill what you were created to do in a way that will separate you from the crowd and bring you before great men.

The ugly stages of life will truly expose who loves you. It will show you who believes in you. It will definitely get rid of the ones who were along just for the free ride. At the beginning of my ugliest stage in life, I'd reconnect with a young lady named Calandra I knew in college. She and I never dated in college. In fact, she was my little sister away from home. Just a cool person. While in college she'd introduce me to girls, and I'd advise her on guys. She was my friend.

My friend, now my wife of almost 20 years, had a very intimate relationship with God. The word intimacy was something that was new to me as it relates to God. In all honesty, the true dynamics of the word relationship, the way I know it now, was new to me. Being that she and I were friends our communication was open. She knew me. She knew the bad me. She knew the good me. As only God would have it, she would be the one to settle me.

Nine months after talking on the phone for the first time in four years, we were married and expecting our first daughter together. She accepted my oldest two children as her own and never once had a run-in with their mothers. "Wow God, this is all you wanted was for me to leave Michigan, be a father to my children, give my life to you, settle down and get married." Never did I consider that God was ordering my steps in preparation for something even bigger. He was putting all of the pieces in the right place.

I was beginning to feel blessed and favored until the bottom fell out during the week of our wedding. The week we got married, I was laid off. I was laid off during the telecom crisis that happened shortly after 9/11. I wouldn't find another job for 2 months. I lost my insurance and cashed in my 401k in order to have money. We applied for welfare assistance the week following our wedding. In most cases, my wife would've been advised not to marry me, a 27-year-old college drop-out, with two children, a pregnant fiancé, and now unemployed. I felt less than a man. Not that she made me feel less than a man but, as a man, I wanted to take care of my family as I'd seen my dad do.

I've left my career of choice. Walked away from what I thought was my purpose. Now I'm in a position unable to provide for the family I've created. Depression was lurking once again. Low self-esteem is beginning to bear fruit. What kind of man have I become? Never once did my wife speak of walking away. In fact, every little thing I did, she cheered and made me feel like it was the best thing ever. She's a good one, I know.

It would be close to three months before I'd land another job. I initially lied about my previous income in hopes to get more. But my spirit has now begun to talk to me a lot more. This thing called integrity was starting to bother me. "Anything you have to lie to get, God didn't give it to you. Anything you have to lie to keep, God already took it from you." With those words being whispered in my spirit, I changed the amount I previously made on the application to the right amount. As expected, they offered me less. But it was better than nothing. I took the job making $31,000/year.

A month after landing the new job, our daughter was born. With a newborn baby, my wife was unable to work, go to school, and take care of the baby. I didn't want that for her. So, for the first five years of our marriage, she was a stay at home mom and later finished college with a Degree in Chemistry in 2006.

Thirty-one Thousand Dollars was a lot of money to us, however, after taxes I'd bring home around $900 every 2 weeks after taxes. Our rent was $750, 2 car notes, insurance, pampers, light bill, groceries. We were barely making ends meet. In fact, our account was negative most of the time with overdraft charges. His will says sell one of the cars, downsize the apartment, find some cheaper car insurance and shop more responsible for groceries. My will said, "Pay day loan." We'd pay $90 per week on a $500 loan. This went on for over 4 years. Ends never met. I was doing things my way.

Even in our mismanagement of our funds, we never went without our needs being met. Six months of being on my job, my performance was reviewed, and I received a performance increase. God would bless my wife's womb again with our fourth child. After eight months on the job I was promoted to another account. This increased my salary to $42,000/year. I begin to see that walking in purpose requires integrity. I begin to see that God didn't need my help blessing me. He needed my obedience. Being where I was supposed to be and doing what I was supposed to do, opened the door for opportunity.

I begin to see other skillsets I had outside of music. I was good at managing people. I was good at listening. I was good at diffusing heated moments. I had a passion for nurturing people and propelling them to do their best. I'm feeling

Often, we mistake process with punishment.

---

positive, but yet I'm behind on my car notes. Doctor bills are coming in. I can't make enough to pay off the payday loan.

I'm supporting a family of six now. Our account was still regularly -$300. Each pay period, I'm writing bad checks to feed my family. Trying to get caught up. We were faithfully tithing every pay period, so I'm not understanding the consistent lack. "God!!!! There has to be more! Why am I being punished? My family deserves so much better."

I can only believe that our foundation of dependency was being laid. God was trying to show me something through the consistency of my wife's faith.

Through it all, my wife never judged me. She never made me feel less than a man because I was unable to provide the way I wanted to. She never disrespected me by comparing me to others.

My wife has always been very soft-spoken and submissive. Her worship has always been pure in my eyes. Often as she walked through the apartment, she'd be singing. One particular Saturday while cleaning and singing something happened. Before I knew it, I heard screaming and crying. I heard high pitched "Thank You Jesus! Lord, you're so worthy! Hallelujah!" I heard an intimate private worship that shook my soul. I sat on the bed and listened. I realized that my wife and God had something serious. More serious than I'd ever had. I realized that God had gifted me with one of His best. I began to wonder "WHY?" Why would God give me someone whose relationship with him is unlike anything I've ever experienced?

I recall hearing in my spirit, "How can you lead a woman like that if you're not as committed to the God she's worshiping?" What God was speaking to me was that my wife was so committed to Him, that she would rather be without me or anyone else if it meant her not having a relationship with Him. She's never spoken this to me, but I know in my heart that she told God, "If he's not the one for me, take him away." She is the type, that would walk away if you tried to come between her and her God.

That morning, I whispered a prayer, "God, I want to know you like that. I'm tired of just existing and going through the motions. I'm tired of struggling. I'm tired God. I don't want to lose anything you've given me." Shortly after that, I stop going to clubs and even stop writing and recording my R&B music. I felt like I needed to grow up and start making God a true priority. At this time, I was willing to try anything to come out of this cave. I surrendered my will for His will.

Power Points of Purpose:

CHAPTER TWELVE

SUBMISSION

There comes a point in your walk with Christ where your faith will be tested. After so many years of ups and downs, God kept my wife and I together. I'd been a member at my church for a few years now. I was wondering and questioning why I was beginning to feel as though God was pressing in my heart that it was time for us to move to another church. I wanted to remain loyal in the place that helped get me back on track and gave me a platform to use my talent. Now that I look back on it, I can say I was becoming more religious than relational. At the time I didn't realize that my spirit and our financial situation mirrored each other. I was spiritually empty, and I was doing whatever I had to do to get by. I could use my skillset and maneuver my way through a service and still walk out spiritually empty. I wasn't applying what was being taught because I was preoccupied using my talent to fulfill my need to be validated by people.

Around 2 am on a Saturday night, the power of God filled our room. My wife and I were watching a young minister on TV. As she preached, there was such power and compassion in her voice that the entire congregation erupted in praise. No music, just pure preaching and praise. I knew this woman knew the Lord. I could see and feel what my wife felt often. I felt what was missing in me. At that moment I knew why it was time to leave our church home. I'd become too familiar and too comfortable in my current spiritual state. There was nothing wrong with my church. There was a different longing in me. I'd performed and used my charisma so long to where I associated being well received and validated by people as my contribution to the Kingdom. God was shifting my focus and clearing the way to my purpose.

The next morning, I spoke with my wife. I told her, "It's time for us to leave our church." She was shocked and felt as though I didn't hear God correctly. I told her that I've been wrestling for a while. I knew God had spoken and it's time to leave. We both loved our church. She told me, "I'm not used to God not speaking to me in the area of the direction He has for my spiritual life. Just give me some time to process this." What she really meant was, "Let me ask God myself!" I didn't have a problem with that because up until now, I leaned heavy on her faith. There's nothing wrong with having someone to lean on, but eventually one day you're going to have to stand on your own.

Within the next few days, she knew I was hearing from God. "So, where are we going?" she asked. "I'm not sure. He hasn't told showed me anything yet" I said. She submitted her will for what she believed was the Will of God through me, her husband. This was more pressure than ever. When your wife trusts the God in you, that kind of trust goes beyond her trust in you as a man, husband, or father. She's depending on you to trust God to lead the family from another realm of faith. Many have such a perverted view of submission. Without submission in some fashion, nothing happens.

    I began to seek direction. I called my dad. He told me in so many words, God is a God of faith. You want Him to tell you where you're going before you decide to trust Him. If He did that, it would require faith in order to move. I had to trust God and believe. We left our church on good terms. We visited a few churches. God planted us in a startup church that was meeting in a hotel. I was brought on as the worship leader. We went from a church of 600 people on a Sunday to roughly 10 people. After the first service, I truly believed that I'd missed God completely. This can't be it.

    All week I rehearsed in my mind how to tell my wife that I think I missed God. I began to seriously doubt if I heard him right. This couldn't be what He moved us for. The next Sunday morning as we pulled into the hotel parking lot, I told my wife, "I think I missed God. This isn't it. I can't do this." "We went from a full band that was locked! To a piano player that only reads music and can't flow. The people aren't into the music. I can't sing and lead this." My wife looked at me and said, "You said, God said it was time to move on. I'll see you inside." She got out of the car, unbuckled the baby and went into the church. I was shocked.

I was being humbled. No crowds, no cheers, no locked music, just my heart and my talent. God removed the cheering section and exposed me to me. "Can you worship when no one is around? Can you give me your all when the attention isn't on you? Will you worship with all of your abilities when no one cares about how well you can sing? Will you write a love song to me, with more passion and intention as you did for others? Will you let me fill the void in your heart? Will you submit to the process?" says the Lord.

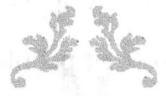

Proverbs 29:11
For I know the plans I have for you,
"declares The Lord," plans to prosper
you and not harm you, plans to give you
hope and a future.

Power Points of Purpose:

CHAPTER THIRTEEN

GOD'S NOT ANSWERING ME

After a tough day at work, I'd often drive around the city just to calm my nerves before going home. I began looking for a second job to try and change our financial situation. I filled out application after application and never received a return call. My wife was totally against me getting a second job because that would leave her with the girls for the entire day alone. Raising children is a full-time job, especially when you have a 1 year old with another on the way. She asked me, "Did God lead you to get another job?" To which I replied, "God's not answering me! I'm tired of struggling. You didn't ask for this. I have to do something." "We'll be ok," she'd say. What I didn't know was, this was beginning to wear on my wife as well. I didn't stop to think that as God was working on me, He was working on my wife as well. For a long time, her faith is what kept us going. As long as she believed in me, I was good.

We would continue on in this rut for a while. We would seek encouragement in any way possible, whether through a TV or Radio ministry. We needed The Word. Sometimes when you're so desperate for change, the enemy picks up on your thirst. He has the tendency to send a misleading word because he's incapable of sending The Word. There's a difference in receiving a word and receiving The Word. Everything God says and does is in order with His Word. As we are sitting watching a televangelist on tv, we're being encouraged that our dark days are over today. Our newness starts right now. Your bills are already paid! Shout! No doubt, we are receiving this word. We prayed and thanked God for paying our bills. This is a true story. We took all of our bills, placed them on the red top barbeque grill and put them on fire! We are burning these bills. It is done! My wife and I locked hands and believed that by this time tomorrow, our bills would mysteriously get paid. We believe. We're faithful at church. We're regular givers, We're good parents. We've suffered long enough. The next month, the same bills came back to our mailbox with different envelopes.

We received and believed that Word. Why didn't it happen? Why isn't God speaking in this part of our lives? I learned that words from God are seeds. He doesn't plant where He's not intending to grow. He plants in seasons. So, there are times He will not answer a valid question because the answer you seek would void the process of what He's trying to teach you.

I'd come home from work one day and my wife was coming downstairs. She was dressed and ready for an interview. At this time, she had not yet completed college. She was just looking for something in order to help out financially. I assume also, to get out of the house in order to have time away to herself. She came and kissed me and said I'll be back. I grabbed the girls, both still in diapers, and said "Where are you going?" "I have to do something. I can't just sit around and watch you do everything you're doing. I have to find a job" she said. I told her, "Baby, you're doing more for this family than you could ever imagine." She said, "But I need to add financially too." I asked her, "Did you talk to God? Did He tell you to go out and find a job?" To which she answered, "No, but I have to do something." She left.

I sat on the floor playing with the girls to keep from breaking down. A few minutes later, I heard the keys at the door. It sounded like fighting on the other side of the door. I got up and opened the door and my wife fell inside the house. Her face was red, and she was gasping for air. I began looking outside because I thought she had been attacked. She finally caught her breath and begin crying. "What's wrong? What happened?" I asked. She then told me, "When I got in the car, I shut the door and locked it. When I got ready to turn the key all of the air in the car seemed to have gotten sucked out. I started suffocating and couldn't breathe. I couldn't open the door. Once I got it opened, I ran back to the house and I didn't catch my breath until I got back in." As tears form in my eyes as I type this, she broke down in my arms. My encourager is now in need of being encouraged. My worries and stress had begun to attack her faith. Let me repeat that, MY WORRIES, and MY STRESS, had begun to attack HER FAITH. Some would look at this like we're about to fall apart, but the exact opposite happened. The switch began to happen as my faith had to step up to help increase her faith. What I didn't know was God was positioning me as the head of my house. Not just in providing, but more importantly in obedience. He was positioning us for purpose.

In all of these crazy financial times, we had no idea that God was building integrity, character, humility, faithfulness, and stewardship. We'd been struggling so long, whenever we did get a little extra, we'd blow it on a good time. We deserved it, so we thought. Not realizing that He who is faithful over a few things would be ruler over many.

Our marriage was built on communication as friends. However, we walked into the marriage backwards with no job, no money, with children, and no degrees. But what we did have sustained us. We had friendship and a purpose. Therefore, as these tough times continued to mount up, it was our communication and friendship that kept us believing. Never once did she blame me, neither did I blame her. It's only because of God we never blamed each other for what we didn't have. We may have wanted to, but it didn't happen.

Finally, breakthrough happened in a weird way. Sure, I know some financial gurus reading had our problems figured out a few pages ago, but remember these were OUR problems. Everyone has struggles that equip them for the purpose they are created to fulfill. Some people just so happen to struggle in an area you may excel in. Struggles strengthen.

In 2005, we filed for bankruptcy. After researching and seeing all of our options, this was the best option for us. We prayed about it and received a simultaneous confirmation. Our debt reduced down to a payment of $258 per month for the next 5 years. We would pay our debt and owe no man nothing. Some people looked down on us. While others understood. What we didn't know was people who own businesses take this route often for a fresh start.

Shortly after filing and beginning payments, we decided to move to another place. My wife went back to college to finish her degree. I recorded my first national gospel project and signed a recording contract.

One weekend, while in Virginia, I asked the Lord, "Why did I have to file for bankruptcy? Why didn't you just send us a check or have someone bless us with the money to pay off our debt?" He replied, "All of these things, I have the power to do. I know the very hairs on your head. It's easy to say what you will do when you don't have it to do it with. Minds change when you have the resources. You asked for a way to be made to pay off your bills, the way was provided and your bills will be paid off over time if you remain faithful to the process." Always a lesson.

Power Points of Purpose:

CHAPTER FOURTEEN

YES?

Still working corporately, we have a little extra money since now the bankruptcy has reduced our debt. My wife decided to finish her degree. Unfortunately, she couldn't take these last six hours in Texas. She would have to go back to Arkansas in order to complete her degree. Initially, our first thought was to postpone it and find other options. During this time, unbeknownst to me, another company had won the contract from the company I'd been working with for five or six years now. I thought my days were over. Not again Lord! I just filed for bankruptcy. On the day of the announcement of our jobs being outsourced to another firm, I went into my office, standing at the door was a lady named Heidi. She was the CEO of the company that had just taken over the contract. She asked could she meet with me. Of course, I'm nervous because the way the last five years have gone, she informed me that her company would be taking over our contract in a few weeks. I knew my company wanted to keep me. They'd already informed me that they would find another position for me. I was comfortable knowing that I would at least have something. I decided to listen to her. She informed me that the contract she just inked was for multiple locations across the country. She wanted every other location to mirror my location. She offered me the job overseeing and implementing every location to the image of what I'd built here locally. My jaw dropped. She offered an $11,000 raise if I took the job. Of course, I KNEW this was God. I immediately called my wife.

This job would require me to travel for about 6 months across the country implementing new policies and procedures that I'd created for my current location. My wife needed to go back to Arkansas for 6 months to finish her degree. This job would afford me the time and the money to take care of my family while traveling. What I didn't know then that I know now, God was teaching me how to build. I would be away from my wife and children off and on for 6 months. He was teaching how to be faithful even when no one is watching. I took the job.

Not only did my contract professionally switch providers, my spiritual walk would take a massive turn shortly after my corporate promotion. For months now, I'd been waking up nightly and hearing, "It's time. Preach My Word." I'd cast it off as just being tired and sleepy. But every night for almost a year, "It's time. Preach My Word." I decided to test the voice. I called my dad and he'd change the topic. He refused to attempt to validate what God was speaking. So, I prayed. "God, for some reason I keep hearing, "It's time. Preach My Word at the same time every night. I've heard many stories on being called and this isn't nearly as dramatic as what I've heard. If this is you, If this is you, Lord please come to me in a dream tonight and speak it to me. If you don't speak tonight, I'll know it's not you." I went on my way to work with no problem. That night I went to bed and slept through the entire night. The next morning, I woke up. I jumped up very excited because I didn't have a dream. I didn't hear the voice. God didn't visit me in my dream. I'm off the hook. As I was ironing my clothes, I was all too happy to praise God. The TV was muted. There was a choir singing on TV. Their motions and emotions were so passionate, I had to hear what they were singing about. I unmuted the TV. The lead singer began to sing, "Go on and do, what He told you to do. Manifest!" At that time, I knew exactly what had just happened. Why did I unmute this TV?

    I'd go to work and not leave my office. After I got home from work, I sat in my favorite seat, poured my favorite drink and cried. I called my parents and expressed to them what happened. "In all things you have a choice son. We always told you, if you can help it, don't do it. The choice is yours if you're going to be obedient. Your purpose found you. You were trying to get me to validate what God was saying. God doesn't need me to validate what He's telling you. If you choose to walk in obedience, God will lead you. If you choose not to, be ready to deal with the consequences of walking outside of your purpose."

I said yes. In 2005 I accepted my calling to preach the Gospel. Shortly after accepting my calling, my wife went back to school and graduated in 2006. In early 2007 after 6 years of marriage, two years into a 5-year bankruptcy, we were approved for a 4-bedroom home with 2.5 bathrooms, 2 living areas, 2 car garage, and a game room. Out of a $7,000 down payment, we paid $647. Yes, $647. Two months later our $647 was returned to us in a refund. Some kind of way our down payment had been fully funded.

It was as if the "Yes" sent a fresh wind and turned the page and closed a chapter that a lot of people may not have survived. But God! When purpose finds you, what will you say?

Power Points of Purpose:

CHAPTER FIFTEEN

PURPOSED CONCEALED

(STOP LEANING)

In the book of Proverbs, you'll find many instructions in the area of wisdom. A very familiar passage encourages us to "Trust in the Lord with all thine heart; lean not unto thine own understanding. In all thy ways acknowledge Him and He shall direct thy paths. (Proverbs 3:5-6). While walking in the why of your existence, it's important to always remember your creator. (Ecclesiastes 12:1). Why is this important? Everything created or made came with instructions from the maker. These instructions are given as directions on how to use or not use a created product. Who better to receive instructions from than the creator?

The scripture says "Trust" meaning believe and or have faith in the Lord with "ALL" thine or your heart. I quoted the word "ALL" because all means all. All means everything. All means the whole amount, quantity, or extent. All means there's nothing left. Lean not to your own understanding: Anything that leans may not be stable. It's incapable of standing on its own. It's shaky or unreliable and can't take much weight. Have you ever sat at a table in a restaurant and the table is rocking? You realize either the foundation is slanted or the legs are unevenly cut. This causes the weight to favor one side over the other. If you're like me, I have a hard time sitting at a table or in a chair that's unstable. My mind wonders, can this table hold the food? Will the food slide? Can this chair hold my weight? Will it break? Leaning is an indication that there's a trust issue. When you lean on your own understanding it exposes a lack of trust in your creator. A lack of trust in any type of relationship is a relationship that may still be in the process of being shaped. We gain trust through opposition. Most of us treat God as if He's let us down. While on the other hand, He treats us as if we've never failed Him. Is it possible for God to have more faith in us that we have in Him? That's something to consider. God has faith in what He placed in us. Before I formed you, I knew you. (Jeremiah 1:5). So, it's not so much that He trusts us as much as He trusts what He put in us. Genesis 1:26 says, "Let us make man in our image, after our likeness." He knows what He put in you.

It's easy to lean to our own understanding. Daily we see things and we try to put things together based off of the information we obtain with our natural minds. However, when you're in position for purpose to find you, you will see things differently. Where others see crisis, you'll see opportunity. Where others see a dead end, you'll see a fresh start. Where others see stagnation, you'll find rest. Where others decide to curse, you'll choose to bless. When others choose to walk away, you'll choose to walk towards. When others choose to complain, you'll choose to trust. Daily we are all faced with similar issues. What makes you different is how you handle them. Through which set of eyes will you view life?

In "ALL" of your ways acknowledge Him and He will direct your path. There that word is again. In ALL of your ways; every step, every direction, every instruction, every thought, every decision, every opportunity "Acknowledge" Him. *The word acknowledge means to recognize the rights, authority, or status of.* In all of your ways, recognize [identify] the rights [privileges], the authority [position], the status [timing/appointed time], and He will direct your path.

Believe or have faith in your creator with all your heart; Don't waver with what you see or think. In all of your thoughts, direction, and decisions, identify Him [Where is God in this? Would He be pleased with this? Will God get the glory out of this?] and He will give you directions on which route to take.

Being God-Confident doesn't mean you don't have confidence in yourself, it means you have as much confidence in you as you have God in you. One day while I was out working, I heard a scripture whispered in my spirit. "Do not put your trust in mere humans. They are as frail as breath. (Isaiah 2:22). I began to internally debate with what I was hearing. "God, I don't put more trust in people than I do you. I pray and seek you for guidance daily." I said. The next instruction I would receive would humble me unlike ever before. He whispered, "Trust in no man. Look in the mirror. What are you?" I agreed. "Lord, I'm a man. I've talked myself out of things. I've talked myself into things. I've disrespected myself. I've lied to myself. I've convinced myself that I wasn't worth your goodness. I've condemned myself. I've talked myself into believing I was alone." It was at that moment that Proverbs 3:5-6 came alive. God was simply telling me when you feel like you can't, God can. When people trust in you, they're not trusting you, they are trusting the God in you. When they see you, do they see God? When they hear you, do they hear God? This is why scripture says:

Philippians 4:13, I can do all things through Christ that strengthens me.

Matthew 19:26, With man it is impossible, but with God all things are possible.

Jeremiah 17:7, But blessed is the one who trusts in the Lord, whose confidence is in Him.

Proverbs 16:3, Commit to the Lord whatever you do, and He will establish your plans.

Psalm 37:5-6 Commit your way to the Lord; trust in Him and He will do this: He will make your righteous reward shine like the dawn, your vindication like the noonday sun.

1 John 3:21-22, Dear friends, if our hearts do not condemn us, we have confidence before God and receive from Him anything we ask, because we keep His commands and do what pleases Him.

Romans 13:1, Let everyone be subject to the governing authorities, for there is no authority except that which God has established. The authorities that exist have been established by God.

When your confidence is in God, you are more cautious with the decisions you make. Your eyes and ears are open to the will of God even if His will draws you away from your own. When your confidence is in God, you are not surprised by the challenges or assignments you are presented with that takes you away from the realm of comfort. When your confidence is in God, you realize when people see and hear you, they see and hear who you represent.

In Judges 6, we find a young man named Gideon who was purposed to do what he thought was impossible. He was chosen to bring the people of Israel out of oppression. The children of Israel were being tormented materially, mentally, and financially by the Midianites, Amalekites, and people from the far east. Whenever Israel would plant crops the people from Midian and Amalek would come and destroy their crop and steal their cattle. The Israelites would hide themselves in caves and mountains just to escape the unfair treatment. Each time the people would make strides, the enemy would come in numbers that couldn't be counted to destroy all they had worked for.

If I were writing a book about then and now, I'd compare this struggle to what a lot of us experience today in a world that oppression is another person's way of staying rich and on top of the world. People that are oppressed live in the caves of depression, anxiety, revenge, and hatred. It's a hard place to escape. The oppressor usually has and has always had more than enough but lives in fear of others growing and surpassing them. One only oppresses what they are in fear of.

Jesus said in Matthew 10:26, The first shall be last and the last shall be first. This statement doesn't have boundaries. As the people of God, we are considered servants of the Most High God. Not servants as in slaves, but servants as in people who live to serve others. We are people who choose to live a life ministering to or helping others. Often the servant is looked down on. Jesus was saying the day is coming when the servant will be looked up to and not down on.

The Israelites cried out to God about the harsh dealings, raids, and theft they were experiencing at the hands of their enemies. They cried out for help. When a nation begins to cry out unto the Lord for help, God will send a prophet. God sent a prophet to Israel. The man of God reminded Israel of how they got into this position. It wasn't that God left them; Israel chose their own will over God's will. Israel is now dealing with the consequences of being out of the will of God. They had leaned on their own understanding. Even though Israel brought this season of oppression on themselves, they were still God's children. Having heard the cries of His children, God sent an angel to speak with the most unlikely young man about a rescue mission.

Gideon was threshing wheat at the bottom of a winepress to hide the grain from the Midianites. The angel of God appeared to him and called him of all things, "Mighty Hero." Gideon was the weakest member of the smallest tribe of Israel. He was voted the least likely to succeed. He wasn't really, but you get the point. He was the least and the last. The angel of God addressed him as a mighty hero and yet Gideon hadn't won a battle. God knew Gideon before He formed Him, therefore God called Him by the name of his finished purpose.

Mighty Hero. Meaning, he, Gideon would be victorious. "Mighty Hero, the Lord is with you!" To which Gideon replied, "If the Lord is with us, why has all this happened to us? And where are all of the miracles our ancestors told us about?" Gideon had heard about all of the miraculous things that God had done in the past. What he is seeing, isn't matching up to what he'd always heard. Gideon didn't realize he was the offspring of people who had rebelled against God. He'd never seen the goodness of God. All of his life he was running from oppressors. All of his life he was used to seeing his enemies prosperous while he and his family suffered. His faith was challenged due to the unfairness of life as he knew it. This is why we as the people of purpose must be sure that we follow the ways of God. We are responsible for future generations. Our children will one day walk in the blessings or curses that we lay before them. If they, like Gideon, are only exposed to the negativity and evil of some of our choices, they too will begin to doubt the goodness of God, as some already have. God sent an angel to the lowliest of the low.

    Understandably Gideon had his doubts. God told him to go in the strength that he had, and he'd rescue the Israelites from the Medianites. Gideon go start a fight with the ones who have been oppressing you. I know you're weak, but I am sending you. If I send you, I'm going to provide for and strengthen you. Gideon was very self-aware. He knew what he was being assigned to do was beyond his own capabilities. Before accepting the assignment, Gideon tested Proverbs 3:6. He acknowledged God (In all of your ways, recognize [identify] the rights [privileges], the authority [position], the status [timing/appointed time], and He will direct your path.)

Gideon said, "If you are truly going to help me [privilege], show me a sign to prove that it is really the Lord speaking to me [identify, authority]. Don't go away until I come back and bring my offering to you." Gideon would leave and prepare a sacrificial offering to present to the angel. How the offering was received would serve as the confirmation that God had spoken to Gideon. The attitude of the giver isn't the only thing important in giving. The actions and the attitude of the receiver also confirm the words that have been received by the giver. The angel of the Lord instructed Gideon on how and where to place the offering. When the offering had been consumed, Gideon knew then it was the angel of the Lord. Gideon knew his purpose.

Gideon would go on to test God 2 other times to make sure he was hearing God right. Each time God reassured Gideon he was the chosen one to complete the task. I'm not going to give you all of the details, I don't want to spoil a good story you can find in the book of Judges chapter 6. I'll just say this, Gideon would go on in the power of the Lord. He would often have to reduce his help to a number of people that most experienced warriors wouldn't dare go to war with. God reduced Gideon's army from 22,000 to 300. God would use less to do more. Gideon would have to trust God with all of his heart and lean not to his own understanding. Because what God would use him to do wouldn't make sense. He followed the path God gave and his purpose through God was fulfilled.

Power Points of Purpose:

CHAPTER SIXTEEN

PURPOSE REVEALED

I was 35 years old when it seemed that things were finally starting to work in my favor financially. I felt as though after accepting my calling to preach my purpose had found me. I was finally in a position to do what I was created to do. Little did I know that as I grew in Christ, every level of growth would cost me to surrender more of myself.

After 3 years of serving as an associate, God begins positioning me for a pastoral assignment. I wasn't eager or excited about this at all. We'd just purchased our new home in miraculous fashion. We moved in in March of 2007. In January 2008, as an alternative to the call I was avoiding, we began what we called family night at our home. I'd cook and invite people over. I'd minister, pray, and serve. We would have an amazing time just being with friends. We would go on to host these meetings on the fourth Friday of every month. The first month I cooked wings and other finger foods. We had 15 people in attendance. The second month I had a fish fry, 30 plus people in attendance. The third month I barbequed, 50 plus people in attendance. On this particular night, God shifted some things that would later present themselves as part of my purpose.

We were all sitting and talking. A young lady began to speak of how God touched her womb. She had been unable to conceive after trying for years. There she sat, after years of trying, with a 6-month-old son. While the conversation was going on, a close relative of mine who drove from hours away to surprise me, got up and walked to the restroom in our bedroom. I went to my room only to hear her crying in the bathroom. I asked her through the door, was she ok? She opened the door and I went in. As she sat on the floor crying with my younger sister and wife now coming into the bathroom, she said, "D, everything that lady out there just said, the doctor just told me last week. I'm unable to have children. The doctor told me there's a blockage in my tubes preventing me from being able to get pregnant. The surgery would cost far too much. I can't have kids." I began to pray for her. Initially, my prayer was for her to be strengthened in order to receive what was spoken by the doctors. But somewhere throughout the course of my prayer, God shifted my prayers.

As I prayed, He reminded me of what the woman had just spoken minutes ago. The evidence of God's final say was laying in his mother's lap asleep. I begin to call her tubes into order through the blood of Jesus. I laid hand on her womb. "God, you created the body. You know exactly how it's supposed to operate. I command in the name of Jesus that these tubes be open."

It was my first time ever stepping out on faith in this nature. I spoke life in her womb believing that God's will would be done. I realized through scripture that not everything we ask and command, in Jesus name, will be granted. Ask the Hebrew Boys, King David, Daniel, and Jesus himself. All were faced with tough situations that I'm sure they wanted to escape but the will of God allowed God to be God and to show Himself strong through the situation. In all cases, God delivered them, but He delivered them in miraculous fashion. Somethings in this life of purpose you're going to have to endure, but you'll never have to endure it alone. God will never operate outside of

1 Corinthians 2:9
Eye has not seen, nor ear heard, Nor have entered into the heart of man the things which God has prepared for those who love Him.

His own will, but we can always choose to operate outside of it. Operating outside of the will of God decreases our chances of operating in the fullness of who were created to be. It also increases our chances of forfeiting what God has prepared for us.

In the fourth month of Family Night, Holy Spirit spoke, "Don't cook. Order Pizza." "Pizza? Lord no one will come if I order pizza." I said. "Exactly!" Out of obedience, I sent out the menu for the upcoming event as I had previously done, to my dismay, the numbers declined drastically. From 50 plus people down to 8 people not including my family of 4. I was sorely disappointed. Holy Spirit revealed to me, "These were the faithful few that were coming for the meat of the Word. This is where you start building my church." We'd eat pizza and talk about the goodness of God for almost 5 to 6 hours. That Friday night in April purpose was being revealed.

A few weeks later, while at work, I receive a phone call. It was my cousin from the third family night. She was crying. I asked "What's wrong?" Me, I figured she was having a moment considering the news the doctor had previously disclosed to her. "I just came from the doctor again. They told me, they don't know how it happened, but my tubes are open. D, I took a pregnancy test, I'm pregnant!" she cried. I could barely contain my composure at work. I screamed in my spirit.

Nine months later, a little guy named Jax was born. A couple of years after that a little lady was born from the same womb. I always knew that God was a miracle worker but, choosing to use me as His vessel was mind-blowing.

Spiritually we were growing but as the economy would have it, my employment status would be challenged again. My contract from my previous job had concluded. We were underbid by yet another competitor. I'd taken another job making at $40,000/year. That's $12,000 less than what I was making prior to moving into our home. My wife was working in her field of study. For the first time in our marital life, we had a two-income household.

Our past experiences with God proved Him to be a provider for us. He just worked a miracle through us. Our faith is stronger than ever. I began praying asking God for provisions to be made for our church. If I'm walking in the purpose He's designed for my life, surely, He's going to provide.

I didn't want to start a ministry to where money was a key focal point. I wanted and needed to help people and restore faith in God. I received word two weeks after our first church service that our office would be closing. My position would be phased out. This time around, I didn't worry. Within the next few days, I'd receive a phone call from my old boss that hired me a few years back after 911. "David Roberson! How the hell are you?" Only LW addresses me this way. "I'm good L. What's good with you?" I said. "We've had the biggest account in the region for a few years. It's been under a month to month for 2 years due to an old manager doing some illegal things. We need to keep this client. We need a new contract. They are giving us 1 year to turn it around. What would it take to get you back over here with us?" Me knowing I needed the job. I knew what I had asked God for. I knew this was my Gideon challenge. I corporately responded, "Hmmm, I'm not sure L. I have a pretty good thing going over here. Can I get back to you on it? How soon do you need an answer?" He needed an answer within the week. I prayed and thanked God for whatever He was doing. The timing was truly God! A few hours later after researching the position, I saw where I could get at least $55,000/yr. for this position. That would put me back where I was prior. I called L back. "LW, how's it going? I thought about your offer. I'd need at least $60,000/year to come back." "Done! Where do I send the offer letter?" L responded back.

To my surprise, I got exactly what I asked for without hesitation. In the back of my mind I was thinking "CRAP, I didn't ask for enough!" I learned then you have not because you ask not.

I couldn't wait to tell the news to my wife. I got home and shared with her that God has provided a way for us to take care of the church financially. By our second month of ministry, my wife and I were fully supporting the church with our increase. Most of what was received financially, we provided. We knew this was the reason/purpose for the promotion. I remember earlier on telling my wife, God gave me this job just so we could take care of the church without worrying about the money. I believe in 5 years, God is going to ask for it back. I told her, I'm not going to get fired, neither will we lose the contract. I'll have to give it back. Those were my exact words.

The church would begin to grow a little in number but spiritually we were beginning to see things of biblical proportions. After 1 year on the job, the contract would be renewed. I'd get a raise and life was good. In 2009, we'd pay off our bankruptcy a little early and purchase our dream SUV, all black Lincoln Navigator. We have a new home, good job, more responsible, a combined six figure income. What a turnaround one simple yes to God can make. I began fasting and praying like never before. Fully fasting water only for 3 and 5 consecutive days each month. Seeking more of God. Although things seemed to be going well in my life, my spirit man was hungry for more. When you are walking in purpose, your hunger for Christ increases in preparation for your next level of impact. I began to pray; Lord give me more of you. I realized by now that more of God meant less of me. God began to press on me that it was time for us to move. Yes, move! Like leave our home kind of move. Leave our home that we could afford. Leave the home we waited patiently for. Leave the home He would give us to start the ministry. He began to show me that we did exactly what we were supposed to do with this home. He gave us a home to start His church.

    I wrestled for weeks before I revealed to my wife what I felt God was speaking. During my period of waiting so many things happened to confirm my hearing. I told my wife what I believed God was leading us to do. In the truest fashion she said, "Are you sure?" "Yes, I believe so." I said. She simply said, "OK. How soon? When should I start bringing boxes home?" I don't know why I expected a different response. I procrastinated the move for close to 6 months. Just believing God would change His mind as He did for Abraham. Didn't happen. The final straw was when someone tried to rob us in broad daylight. They kicked the door in. All of the church equipment was at our home. We were still hosting bible study in our home. People we'd never met would come to our home for bible class. So needless to say, people had their eye on us. They knew our work schedule. We could be seen loading and unloading every Sunday. Our peace was gone. We had the door replaced and had choir rehearsal while the door was being prepared. Many of the members had the opportunity to watch while all of these things were unfolding. How we handled it as leaders would prove to be valuable later on in ministry. Shortly after the attempted break-in, we woke up to gun shots at a home behind us. It's time to go.

We begin bringing boxes home. We secured a 900 square foot apartment that would be closer to my job. We'd downsize from 2,700 square feet to 900 square feet. Everything we were unable to put into our 900 sq. ft apartment, we gave away to our church family. We gave away furniture sets, a refrigerator, washer/dryer, living room table sets, and full bedroom sets. With the natural eye it would seem as though we were back where we started 9 years ago in an apartment. Our home would go back on the market. Being that my obedience was delayed, our home foreclosed. I believe with all my heart, my delayed obedience caused us to be out of the will of God in this area and we missed out on the sell.

After being in an apartment for a year, we'd find a home to rent that was slightly larger than the apartment. I'd win Manager of the Year and receive an all-expenses paid trip to the Great Exuma Bahamas. My account was thriving so much to the point that we took over other departments and secured another contract. I was promoted yet again. My salary would reach $73,000/year. Not bad for a college drop out with purpose. What I didn't know was God was preparing me for the absolute biggest mental and emotional challenge of my ministry life.

I was sacrificing my personal relationship with God for a working relationship with God.

Within 2 years of being corporately successful, I was beginning to lose my hunger for more because I had enough. A true relationship with God never leaves you empty; it creates new paths for more. I was sacrificing my personal relationship with God for a working relationship with God.

When you are walking purpose, your personal relationship with God is what opens the portal of trust. When God puts his trust in you as a person, He's trusting that you trust Him enough not to try and make it on your own. A lot of times people in leadership forget that it's not our work in ministry that brings us into relationship with Christ, it's our relationship with Christ that brings us our work. I got lost in the work and begin feeling like my work was justifying my blessing and my position. When Jesus said in <u>Matthew 7:22-23, Many will say to me I that day, 'Lord, Lord, did we not prophesy in your name and in your name drive out demons and in your name perform many miracles?' Then I will tell them plainly, 'I never knew you. Away from me, you evildoers!</u>' He was saying, you can do the work, but if I don't have a personal relationship with you, how then can I say I know you personally. I realized that my personal relationship with Christ was the entry point to my purpose. There are people that worked for me for years, whom I never knew. They did what I needed them to do, received a check and went home. If the day ever came and they showed up at my home, I'd turn them away because I didn't have a personal relationship with them.

  I went through a period where I was being humbled yet again. After having a great job, making good money, I'd began building the ministry according to what I saw and not what I was hearing. I became so musically driven to where my time in the Word was minimal compared to my time at music rehearsal. I'd hire good musicians. Work with great singers. I worked hard trying to be there for everyone. I believed with all my heart I was in God's will because I am writing songs and building what I thought was His church. I was losing track of who I was created to be and almost fell back into who I used to be. My financial security was giving me a false sense of where my relationship truly was with God. I'd become comfortable in ministry. God's purpose for me was much more than I had envisioned. I felt myself increasing and my dependency on God decreasing. By now I've become spiritually aware when something is spiritually unbalanced, I've learned to stop and Proverbs 3:5-6.

I have a passion in my heart to see people grow and change. I wanted more of God in order to lead His people in the manner He designed. I didn't want to go through the motions and live on an emotional high from week to "weak.". I wanted my faith to be real.

Midway through my fifth year of employment since starting the church, God begins to speak those words in my heart again, "It's time to move. It's time to live by the faith you teach about."

My purpose would cost me my $73,000/year job. How and who in their right mind would walk away from $73,000/year to lead a ministry that depends heavily on what they contribute? I begin thinking, maybe it's just time for me to leave this job. Maybe it's just time for a new challenge? This time, I spoke with my wife early on. "How long have you been working there babe?" she said. "A little over five years," I said. She said, "Do you remember when you first got the job you said that God would ask you for it back after about 5 years." I had completely forgotten about that.

I took a couple of days off to pray and just get my thoughts together. I decided to put my resume out, just in case it was just time for me to leave that particular location. I received a phone call from a guy named Robert. Robert asked for an interview. That Friday I drove over to McKinney to meet with Robert about placing me with another company. I'm pretty sure by now this is what God was saying. Robert would call me back to his office and we'd begin the interview. "I could place you pretty easy but I'm curious as to why you're trying to leave your job. It looks like they've been good to you and you've worked out for them." He said something along those lines. I stated to him that I was looking for something different because I'm at the level of employment to where I can't be promoted without being promoted into something regional. I told him I didn't want to travel. He asked, "Why not?" "I have a wife and children. I have no desire in seeing them sparingly. I also, pastor a church I'm trying to grow and me being away would take too much time away from that as well." At this point for the first time Robert makes eye contact with me. He said, "You're a Pastor?" I said, "Yes sir." I began talking about the church and I suppose my life lit up while I was talking about it. He looked at me and said, "You already have a job." Tears began to roll down his face. This is someone I've never seen or talked to in my life. "You don't know how bad I don't want to help you right now," he said. "I get a 30% commission from your salary if I place you, but that 30% wouldn't do me any good. People in this world need what you have. Go home and talk to your wife and let me know what I can do to help you make this transition, Pastor." By this time, I'm fighting back tears. What was scheduled as a job interview turned in to confirmation for a job in view. That day Robert's purpose was to confirm what I'd heard. I couldn't deny what God was leading me to do.

The following Monday in December of 2012, I went to work and submitted my resignation effective February 2013. I knew it would take them time to replace me, so I stayed long enough to train my replacement. I passed the baton. For the first time in my life I was totally dependent on God. I walked away from my job to pastor the church on a full-time basis. At the time our church wasn't in the position to replace my income. My leaving corporate America would decrease our total household income by close to 70%.

I thought about downsizing our car. We considered going back to an apartment. With each thought of downsizing, the Lord said "No. Keep everything you have. I will provide."

A few months after going full-time in ministry our lease would expire. We would move to an even bigger home closer to the church. Right before our eyes the church began to grow physically, financially, and most important spiritually.

I often wondered why I had to walk away from my dreams and so many materialistic things in order to deepen my relationship with God. God wanted to prove to me that He was the giver of all things. When you are a leader, there comes a time when you desire more. Enough isn't always enough. What God revealed to me later on, as I continued this walk of faith, was that people can still get lost with written directions. He reminded me of the trips the church takes together. With over 20 cars trailing me, I'd have to slow down at each light just to make sure every car behind me made it through. Yes, sure everyone had GPS, but there are times when GPS offers an alternate route to avoid traffic. Not all traffic is bad. Some traffic actually slows you down for a reason.

As a leader, I began to realize that some people do better in life having someone they can follow in view. When the leader is so far ahead of the people he's responsible for, distractions come more frequently. Once you lose traction, you're spinning in the same puddle of mud until someone pulls you out. The devil can't stop your purpose but if he can distract you, he can delay your arrival.

I told you a portion of my story in order for you to realize that the same God that gave purpose to Hannah's closed womb, Eli's position as priest, Samuel prophetic gift, David's anointed rocks, and Gideon courageous testing, is the same God that's at work in you right now. We often forget that we are the people God has chosen to use in this generation. We often pursue validation from our peers, not realizing that sometimes another's validation or lack thereof is because they may be in competition.

After leaving my job for full-time ministry, I was talked about. I was doubted. I even doubted myself and thought I'd missed God on several occasions. Many people were of the mindset, "God gave you that job, He wouldn't take it back." To which I'd reply, He didn't take it back, He asked for it and I gave it. Don't get discouraged because you're not easily understood. Your purpose isn't for everyone to understand. When God is in control, your path will always set the platform for your arrival. You are God's transportation to a world in need of mercy for survival.

Some may want to know, what did I get in place of it? Matthew 19:29 was the scripture of promise and purpose that brought me peace and continues to bring me peace to this day.

I can't even begin to tell you what God has done in my life that money can't buy. Yes, He replaced and increased our income. Yes, He replaced our home with another one that we built. However, the most important part of walking in purpose is found in Matthew 6:33, "Seek ye first the KINGDOM and His righteousness and all of these things will be added to you. Yes, the things may have been added but God knows that things will not separate us from Him. He knows that He's our priority. We know that it's because of Him that we live and move and have our being.

Matthew 19:29
"And everyone who has left houses or brothers or sisters or fathers or mothers or wife or children or fields for my sake will receive a hundred times as much and will inherit eternal life."

As I've walked in my purpose, I've been allowed to be used as a vessel to lay hands on many who were barren, and they've brought new life into the world. I've been used to pray over people on life support and they've coughed up the tubes. I've seen impure spirits flee. I've been given the opportunity to speak to someone over the phone who was in a coma on life support. She had passed earlier in the day, but the doctors were able to resuscitate her. We walked her through the prayer of salvation as she was unresponsive, I believed she could hear us. As we spoke to her, "If you believe that Jesus Christ is the son of God and that He died and rose again for your sins, you are saved." At that moment a tear fell down the lady's face while she lay in a coma. A few hours later, she went home to be with Jesus.

Never had it crossed my mind that God would plan such a purposeful life for me. To see Him work is something that I look forward to on a daily basis. When you embrace what you don't know and believe and receive what God knows, you'll find that God already knew everything your learning about yourself. As you walk in your purpose your availability to God or lack thereof will either open your eyes or keep you blind to who you really are in Christ.

Before He formed you, in the womb, He already knew you. You're not behind. You're just getting started!

Power Points of Purpose:

Other available resources by **David D. Roberson**

 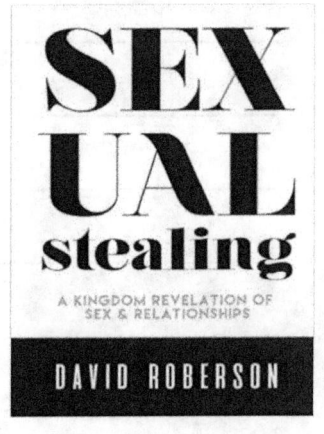

www.ingramcontent.com/pod-product-compliance
Lightning Source LLC
Chambersburg PA
CBHW071456080526
44587CB00014B/2125